Consuelo A. Bundy

WALKING In WISDOM

A Woman's Workshop on Ecclesiastes

Books in this series—

WALKING In WISDOM

A Woman's Workshop on Ecclesiastes

Barbara Bush

Lamplighter Books Grand Rapids, Michigan

Zondervan Publishing House

WALKING IN WISDOM: A WOMAN'S WORKSHOP ON ECCLEASTIES
Copyright © 1982 by The Zondervan Corporation
Grand Rapids, Michigan

Lamplighter Books are published by Zondervan
Publishing House, 1415 Lake Drive, S.E.,
Grand Rapids, Michigan 49506

Library of Congress Cataloging in Publication Data

Bush, Barbara.
    Walking in wisdom.

    Bibliography: p.
    1. Bible. O.T. Eccleasties—Criticism, interpretation, etc.   I. Title.
BS1475.2.B87   1982   223'.806   82-17436
ISBN 0-310-43041-0

All scripture quotations, unless otherwise noted, are taken from the HOLY
BIBLE: NEW INTERNATIONAL VERSION (North American Edition). Copyright
© 1973, 1978, 1984, by The International Bible Society. Used by permission of
Zondervan Bible Publishers.

Edited by John Iwema

Printed in the United States of America

85   86   87   88   89   90   91 / 12   11   10   9   8   7   6   5   4

For Dick,
my very own Preacher,
and all the other teachers
who have over the years
so faithfully taught me God's Word

CONTENTS

PREFACE

This study of Ecclesiastes is intended to help individuals and study groups discover how God can use the wisdom He presents in the Book of Ecclesiastes to make us wiser today.

In many cases study groups consist of both Christians and non-Christians, so I have not set out to write a technical study. However, it does seem important that I speak to one matter of controversy concerning Ecclesiastes: the question of authorship.

Until the middle of the nineteenth century, both Jewish and Christian scholars accepted this book of the Bible as the writing of King Solomon. But by that time liberal scholars had begun applying higher criticism to many biblical writings and had concluded that, for example, Moses did not write the Pentateuch, that several other books (such as Isaiah and some of the gospels) were collaborative efforts, and that many books were written at dates later than previously thought. For the most part, conservative scholars debated these findings, although in some cases they joined with liberal scholars in their views. This has been the case with regard to the authorship of Ecclesiastes: conservative scholarship is divided on the issue. Therefore, I will state briefly the main problems involved in this question and my reasons for holding to Solomon as the author of Ecclesiastes.

While the author of Ecclesiastes is nowhere identified by name, the book tells us he was the son of David and king in Jerusalem (1:1); that he was involved in massive building projects (2:4–6); that he exceeded all others in wisdom and wealth (1:16; 2:9); that he spoke in proverbs (12:9; cf. 1 Kings 4:32); and that he had opportunities for tasting all life had to offer as did no other king in Israel's history (2:1 ff.).

Scholars who discount Solomon as author of Ecclesiastes believe the book was written at a much later date, some say as late as 200 B.C., compared to Solomon's B.C. reign in the tenth century. They hold that the book is the work of an unknown writer who used the figure of Solomon as a literary device so that the message of the folly of mere human efforts would be presented in the strongest manner possible.

The crux of the problem in dating Ecclesiastes lies in the language used in the book. Gleason Archer, a respected Old Testament scholar and an evangelical, says in his *Survey of Old Testament Introduction* (1964), "It is undeniably true that the language of the work is markedly different from all that of other tenth-century Hebrew texts which have been preserved in the Bible. For that matter, it is different from all the other books of the Old Testament of whatever age, with the partial exception of the Song of Solomon."

The language difficulties spring from the many words in Ecclesiastes that have been identified as coming from Aramaic roots, forms not commonly found in other literature until nearly the time of the New Testament. However, it is significant that the Song of Songs does use some of these word forms. Also, other scholars hold that most of these roots are not Aramaic at all, but Canaanite-Phoenician.

Neither influence would necessarily rule out Solomon as author. Aramaic was a universal language that was spoken crossculturally for centuries. Laban spoke it (see the Aramaic name in Gen. 31:47), and was in fact referred to as an Aramean (31:24). Other books of the Old Testament also contain portions written in that language.

In addition, Solomon was a sophisticated world figure exposed to numerous cultures (1 Kings 4:34). King Hiram of Phoenicia was a close friend of both David and Solomon (1 Kings 5:1), and 30,000 Hebrews lived in Phoenicia for a period of time in order to obtain cedar and other materials for building the temple, while Phoenician workers also came to Jerusalem (1 Kings 5:12–14; 7:13ff.).

If some modern scholars doubt that Solomon was the author, those closest to the scene, the Jews who assembled the Old Testament canon, made their opinion clear when they placed Ecclesiastes squarely between the two books that do specifically name him as author, Proverbs and Song of Songs. The rules of biblical interpretation hold that the judgment of those closest to the time of the event recorded in Scripture (the earliest manuscripts, etc.) carries the greatest weight. So the fact that the Jews, so careful in transcribing the Scriptures, held Solomon to be the author is a telling point.

The Book of Proverbs begins: "The proverbs of Solomon son of David, king of Israel: for attaining wisdom and discipline; for understanding words of insight" (1:1–2). The book of Ecclesiastes begins: "The words of the Teacher, son of David, king in Jerusalem." Therefore, in this study we will accept the Book of Ecclesiastes as a continuation of Solomon's established role as a teacher of godly insight.

SUGGESTIONS FOR GROUP USE

Choose a meeting place suitable to the type and size of group you will have. This can be a Sunday school classroom or home, or other place that meets your needs. If the group is to meet in a home, it might be best to find one other than that of the leader. It is hard to turn people out of your own home when class is over, but the leader can encourage group members to leave on time by leaving someone else's home at the agreed-on time. And it is easier to secure a hostess for any group if she knows people will leave promptly.

Set a time schedule for class sessions and stick to it faithfully. If coffee or other refreshments are served (this is not a necessity), include this in the schedule, but be sure that the lesson period starts and ends on time. It is the responsibility of the leader to keep faith with group members in the matter of time.

Approach each phase of building a study group prayerfully. Pray that God will guide your decisions, bring the right women to your group, give you wisdom as you study the material, give you a love for each woman, and open each heart to His truth.

The leader may want to open each lesson with a presentation emphasizing material from the book or drawn from other sources (current newspaper and magazine articles or other books) before beginning the group discussion. The Scripture passages under consideration should be read aloud by the leader or a group member, and Scripture references not written out in the text should be looked up by the group members and read aloud as they come up for discussion. During group discussion the leader should keep things moving so that all questions are covered by the end of the allotted time.

Quiet women should be drawn into the discussion whenever possible and can even be asked to answer specific questions so that more talkative women do not overpower them. However, questions that are more personal in nature (as opposed to those which have a specific answer from Scripture) should be answered only by volunteers. In addition to the questions at the end of the chapter, the leader might ask, "Which part of the chapter interested you the most?" or "Which question was the most thought-provoking?"

Encourage the women to personalize the topic of the week so that the study does not become merely an intellectual exercise. Close each class session with an opportunity for group members to commit some area of their lives to the Lord. If they would like to share with the group what that commitment is, they should do so, but no one should feel pressured to make a public statement. The leader may use questions such as the following:

Has the lesson revealed a specific area in your life that needs attention?

Are you willing to change your opinions about how to find meaning in life and bring them in line with God's Word?

Is the Lord prodding you to take some particular action, to obey Him in some specific way?

The leader should then close in a prayer of dedication.

Getting the Group Started

This book can be used by individuals or in group situations. A group should plan to meet for twelve or thirteen weeks. If the first session is used to get acquainted and pass out materials and you would like to keep the study to twelve weeks, chapters 10 and 11 can be done in a single week, since they are shorter and their subjects are compatible.

The first session is a good time to set a few ground rules in as friendly a manner as possible. These might include:

1. We will keep to our schedule, starting and ending on time.
2. Group members are asked to commit themselves to being prepared for each session, studying thoroughly the assigned chapter and answering all the "Finding The Meaning" questions.
3. During discussion, unless the question calls for a personal opinion, we will avoid statements that start with "I think" or "I feel." Instead, we will try to share what God is saying in the Bible.
4. Group members are encouraged to pray for one another and for the leader.

Biblical quotations in the text of the study are from the New International Version. The leader will need to be alert to any confusion caused by different translations being used by group members. You may want to encourage the women to use versions other than the Living Bible, since it is a paraphrase and so its wording is substantially different from major translations of the Bible. Encourage the women to keep their Bibles open during discussion so that versions and answers can be compared without wasting time.

1

SOLOMON SEZ

Ecclesiastes 1:1–18

Pretend you are someone from another world who has landed on earth. You do not know anything about the living creatures you see about you. You do not know anything about God. The only way you can learn about earth people is by watching them and listening to them, comparing how one person acts as opposed to another, and noting how people react in various situations. What conclusions would you draw?

You watch a baby be born, grow up, work, and die. You observe how people spend the money they receive for their labors. You make a note of what makes them laugh and cry. You see them jockeying for position, rank, and honor. You see that some humans toil endlessly, while others never seem to work at all. Some people spend much free time jogging around the same streets day after day, while others sit in a chair and watch images on a screen. Eating seems to be a continuous activity. Inevitably, you ask yourself, "What does it all mean?"

This is the task Solomon set for himself in the Book of Ecclesiastes, the "Book of the Preacher [or Teacher]." He says, "I, the Teacher, was king over Israel in Jerusalem. I devoted myself to study and to explore by wisdom all that is done under heaven" (vv. 12–13). His conclusion is this: "'Meaningless! Meaningless!' says the Teacher. 'Utterly meaningless! Everything is meaningless'" (v. 2). "I have seen all the things that are done under the sun; all of them are meaningless, a chasing after the wind" (v. 14).

Solomon gives reasons for this pessimistic conclusion. Generations come and go (v. 4); the sun rises, sets, then hurries back and starts all over again (v. 5); the wind blows south a while, then turns to the north (v. 6); streams pour into the ocean but never fill it (v. 7); what has been done before is done again and again (v. 9); and the masses of humanity die unremembered (v. 11). Life is like a treadmill on which people expend all their energies only to stay in the same place.

Solomon's Credentials

King Solomon was in a unique position to assess the world and the ways of men. For when he ascended the throne of Israel after his father David, and God promised to give him anything he desired, Solomon asked for wisdom for governing and for distinguishing right from wrong. God was pleased with Solomon's request, and said, "Since you have asked for this and not for long life or wealth for yourself, nor have asked for the death of your enemies but for discernment in administering justice, I will do what you have asked. I will give you a wise and discerning heart, so that there will never have been anyone like you, nor will there ever be. Moreover, I will give you what you have not asked for—both riches and honor—so that in your lifetime you will have no equal among kings" (1 Kings 3:11–13). So Solomon was able to evaluate the worth of wisdom, riches, and honor as one who had tasted it all, and who had the insight necessary to come to correct conclusions in a way a poor man might not.

Understanding Life

But even Solomon found that trying to make sense out of life without God as the great reference point was heavy going. He exclaims, "I devoted myself to study and to explore by wisdom all that is done under heaven. What a heavy burden God has laid on men!" (v. 13). People today have the same problem. Any line of inquiry sooner or later leads to unanswerable questions, to blank walls, to areas incomprehensible to the human mind. If God is not in the equation, our efforts to understand what we see around us are burdensome.

Things *do* seem upside down as we look around us. We see fools in high position and deserving people in low ones (10:6), or those who don't work driving around in the latest sports car while working people take the bus (10:7). A righteous man dies young, but a wicked man prospers (7:15). Anyone trying to draw proper conclusions about life will surely be confused by such evidence.

This is because man is time-bound. He cannot see the big picture. He can look back into history to some extent, but "who can tell him what will happen under the sun when he is gone?" (6:12). He does not see the final resolution of events on earth. And he does not understand the workings of God in the hereafter, unless God reveals this to him (1 Cor. 2:9–10).

Roots of Human Philosophies

The Book of Ecclesiastes, then, is largely an examination of life by a brilliant human being who, by his own admission, attempts to come to grips with the meaning of life without turning to God for enlightenment. It's understandable that the result is confusion, and this confusion is mirrored in the various philosophies that have been espoused down through the ages. As Solomon attests, "What has been done will be done again; there is nothing new under the sun. Is there anything of which one can say, 'Look! This is something new'? It was here already, long ago; it was here before our time" (vv. 9–10).

Much in the philosophies we see today is but a rehash of ancient thinking. For example, there is nothing older than the "new morality." The avant-garde of every age is in reality woefully behind the times. Each generation refines or rebels against the ideas handed down to it, the cycles continuously repeating themselves.

Under the Sun, Above the Sun

Solomon, however, does know God, and although he tries to limit himself to what human intellect can discover, his regenerated mind demands to be heard from time to time. Though he spends most of his time reasoning as a man "under the sun," he occasionally expresses the viewpoint that comes from above the sun, where the Lord dwells. For this reason, attempts to separate Solomon's human wisdom from his supernaturally acquired wisdom require special care on the part of those who want to learn what God is teaching us in the Book of Ecclesiastes. The readers of Ecclesiastes need the Holy Spirit to reveal truth to them (John 16:13) so that they will be able to handle God's Word correctly (2 Tim. 2:15).

If you have never received Jesus Christ into your life, the Bible will make little sense to you. "The man without the Spirit does not accept the things that come from the Spirit of God, for they are foolishness to him, and he cannot understand them, because they are spiritually discerned" (1 Cor. 2:14).

This spiritual discernment does not come naturally with age or from human effort. As Jesus said, "Flesh gives birth to flesh, but the Spirit gives birth to spirit. You should not be surprised at my saying, 'You must be born again' " (John 3:6–7). When you ask Jesus Christ into your life you become God's child, you are born into His spiritual family (John 1:12–13). Then, with the Holy Spirit dwelling within you, you can begin to understand what God is saying in the Bible (1 Cor. 2:12). It will no longer be a dry, confusing book to you because with your new spiritual eyes you will discern truth that you couldn't see with your natural eyes. If you have never done so, stop reading now and ask Jesus to come into your heart and make you clean from your sins so that you can receive and understand God's Word.

We must remember, though, that everyone, whether a new believer or a mature Christian, needs to approach the study of Scripture in an attitude of prayer. We need to pray with the psalmist, "Open my eyes that I may see wonderful things in your law" (119:18). As Solomon pleased God by asking for wisdom, so will we today as we approach His Word. He says, "Call to me and I will answer you and tell you great and unsearchable things you do not know" (Jer. 33:3).

* * * *

FINDING THE MEANING

1. Read the twelve short chapters of Ecclesiastes and mark these words and phrases each time you find them: "meaningless" (in some translations "futile" or "futility," "vain" or "vanity"), "under the sun," and "striving [chasing] after wind."

2. Why is "chasing after wind" a good description of "futility"? <u>see verse 2:11 . Wind is always changing</u> 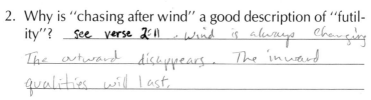 <u>The outward disappears. The inward</u> <u>qualities will last.</u>

3. Can you think of modern-day examples of people "chasing after the wind"? <u>Workaholic, self-gratification, approval of others, searching for spiritual without application</u>

4. When you pretended to be an alien at the beginning of the chapter, what did you notice about the lives of people? <u>Repititive, did unimportant things. Inconsistent; words vs actions</u>

5. Have you asked Jesus Christ to come into your life? If not, is there any good reason why you should not do so now?

2

THE TROUBLE WITH PLEASURE

Ecclesiastes 2:1–3

When children are given some money, what is their first impulse? To put it in the bank? To give it to someone less fortunate? Usually not. They are most likely to head for the ice cream or candy counter, or find a vending machine full of plastic junk. The basic tendency of every human being is to use his or her resources to seek immediate personal pleasure.

We should not be surprised then that Solomon first turns to hedonism as he seeks to find out what has meaning in life. "I thought in my heart, 'Come now, I will test you with pleasure to find out what is good'" he says (v. 1). But what is understandable in a child seems shockingly shallow as the first recourse of the wise king of Israel. His blatant admission that he is setting out to seek physical gratification is embarrassing—until we finish the verse and find Solomon telling us ahead of time, "But that also proved to be meaningless."

Laughter

"Having a good time" is practically the cult religion of our day. Do you remember your high school or college days? Learning often seemed inconsequential; having a good time appeared to be the major goal. Do you recall how necessary it was to be laughing all the time? The "fun" girls were the popular ones; a serious-minded person was a "drag." You were expected to explode with laughter at the most asinine stories or practical jokes, or else be considered a social flop. But Solomon says, "Like the crackling of thorns under the pot, so is the laughter of fools. This too is meaningless" (7:6).

Our "comedies" on television come out of the same mentality that ruled our adolescence. If writers and actors cannot get live audiences to respond well, pre-taped laugh tracks keep the viewers at home fooled into thinking the show is hilarious. Everything is amusing these days: adultery, drunkenness, rebellious children, homosexuality, fornication amongst teen-agers—all are presented with quips, double-takes, and giggles. Thus we find ourselves snickering at the very things God condemns, just as we did in our high school days, proving the truth of Romans 1:32: "Although they know God's righteous decree that those who do such things deserve death, they not only continue to do these very things, but also approve of those who practice them."

How much of our laughter is a joyous response to the goodness of the life God has provided for us, and how much is a forced effort to convince ourselves and others that we are having a good time, that we are a fun person to be with? "Laughter," Solomon says, "is foolish. And what does pleasure accomplish?" (2:2).

In a society that wants us to have fun at all costs, people are forced to go around like court jesters or clowns, with grins plastered on their faces in a continuous effort to look cheerful, while hiding hearts hungry for more satisfying human contact.

In Proverbs 14:13 we read: "Even in laughter the heart may ache." If someone's heart is breaking, what does such laughter accomplish?

Stimulants

In our school days, as now, such continuous boisterousness is impossible to sustain without reinforcement. So the next step is the same in our culture as it was for Solomon: "I tried cheering myself with wine, and embracing folly" (v. 3). While we can believe Solomon when he says he did this while his mind was guiding him wisely (v. 3), that is not the motivation of others.

Why does the world think that liquor or drugs are absolutely essential to the success of a party? Isn't it, as Solomon says in Proverbs 31:7, so they can "forget their poverty and remember their misery no more," and enter into superficial laughter? Isn't it considered amusing to hear about someone drinking someone else under the table? Aren't those who have a large capacity for liquor still admired, even though Isaiah 5:22 says, "Woe to those who are heroes at drinking wine and champions at mixing drinks"?

The world equates having a good time with consuming intoxicating beverages. That was even the immediate judgment of some who saw the disciples on the Day of Pentecost, when the Holy Spirit was given to the church. "Some, however, made fun of them and said, 'They have had too much wine'" (Acts 2:13). It is unbelievable to the world that a person can have real fun without using some sort of stimulant. They do not understand that Christ came so that our joy might be complete and satisfying rather than artificial and temporary (John 15:11). Peter quotes from the Old Testament (Ps. 16:8–11) to explain to the observers that they were not drunk—after all, it was only nine in the morning—but that when God's Spirit is present, true delight abounds.

The church my husband pastors traditionally has a communion service at 11:00 P.M. on New Year's Eve in order to usher in the new year in an attitude of prayer. After one of these services, a young woman said to me, "This was such a special time. It's hard to believe that just a few years ago I thought it was the height of fun and excitement to stand out in the street at midnight banging pots and pans and kissing other people's husbands."

Drink helps us to "have a good time" by lowering our inhibitions, causing us to act as we never would when sober. "Wine is a mocker and beer a brawler" (Prov. 20:1), and any who indulge in it for very long will find themselves "embracing folly," and even risking disintegration and death.

Sexual Pleasure

It is surprising that in his pursuit of pleasure Solomon has little to say about sexual gratification. Perhaps his honesty required him to admit that his wisdom did not control his sex life as it did his other behavior. The Bible tells us that Solomon's lust and his desire to cement alliances with foreign nations caused him to disobey the Lord's command by taking foreign wives. His indiscriminate pursuit of this kind of pleasure had predictable results: "As Solomon grew old, his wives turned his heart after other gods, and his heart was not fully devoted to the LORD his God, as the heart of David his father had been" (1 Kings 11:4).

As with all pleasure sought outside the will of God, Solomon's liaisons soured in the end. His lack of reconciliation to God in this matter is revealed in the attitude toward women found in Ecclesiastes:

> I find more bitter than death the woman who is a snare, whose heart is a trap and whose hands are chains. The man who pleases God will escape her, but the sinner she will en-

snare. . . . I found one upright man among a thousand, but not one upright woman among them all (7:26, 28).

Solomon has much more to say about the dangers of seeking sexual pleasure in the wrong places in the Book of Proverbs (2:16–19; 6:20–35; 7:6–27). He warns that those who indulge in such activity are "like an ox going to the slaughter, like a deer stepping into a noose till an arrow pierces his liver, like a bird darting into a snare, little knowing it will cost him his life" (Prov. 7:22–23). The biblical name for this is "fornication" if unmarried and "adultery" if married, and God repeatedly warns us of the dire consequences of such actions.

In the Song of Songs, the king explores the joy and delight of sexual love in marriage as it is approved by God. But in Ecclesiastes Solomon reminds us that even within marriage the satisfaction of our sexual desires and intimate companionship will not by themselves give us fulfillment. "Enjoy life with your wife, whom you love, all the days of this meaningless life that God has given you under the sun—all your meaningless days" (9:9).

Food

We learn in 1 Kings 4:22–23 that in order to keep his court going, Solomon's daily provisions included 185 bushels of flour, 375 bushels of meal, 10 head of stall-fed cattle, 20 pasture-fed cattle, 100 sheep and goats, plus deer, gazelles, roebucks, and choice fowl!

Certainly Solomon must have found true pleasure in eating with such delicacies as this, and a land flowing with milk and honey besides! But that is not the case. On the contrary, he concludes, "All man's efforts are for his mouth, yet his appetite is never satisfied. . . . Better what the eye sees than the roving of the appetite. This too is meaningless, a chasing after the wind" (6:7, 9).

Food *does* often look better than it tastes, and we *do* often eat from appetite rather than hunger. Our eating can stem from a desire to give ourselves pleasure rather than from need. The result is an overweight population, and even discomfort: "The full stomach of the rich man does not allow him to sleep" (5:12 NASB). Unfortunately, Christians are often guilty of excess in eating. We don't want to appear to be negative about everything, and overeating seems innocent enough when compared to drunkenness and illicit sex. If we look at some churches, we might even conclude that the Bible said, "Where two or three are gathered in my name, serve food"!

However, all our bodily appetites are to be under control. Solomon warns, "Do not join those who drink too much wine, or gorge themselves on meat" (Prov. 23:20). Gluttony is condemned in Scripture (Prov. 28:7) and will harm our Christian testimony. As Paul says, "No, I beat my body and make it my slave so that after I have preached to others, I myself will not be disqualified" (1 Cor. 9:27).

Endless Craving

The life of the hedonist is a life of endless desire, of constantly looking for new ways to satisfy our numerous bodily cravings. Such quests inevitably draw the seeker away from God and often lead him or her into every fleshly excess (Rom. 1:24ff.). Even for those who keep their pursuit of pleasure within the bounds of traditional morality, Satan, who is the great deceiver, will leave his promises of satisfaction unfulfilled. This is because it is actually beyond the power of the devil to give true pleasure, as C. S. Lewis explains in his *Screwtape Letters*. In this book the veteran demon, Screwtape, writes a series of letters to his neophyte nephew tempter, Wormwood, in order to help him ensnare his victim, and warns:

Never forget that when we are dealing with any pleasure in its healthy and normal and satisfying form, we are, in a sense, on the Enemy's ground. I know we have won many a soul through pleasure. All the same, it is His invention, not ours. He made the pleasures; all our research so far has not enabled us to produce one. All we can do is to encourage the humans to take the pleasures which our Enemy has produced, at times, or in ways, or in degrees, which He has forbidden.[1]

Screwtape is, however, able to encourage Wormwood:

As this condition becomes more fully established you will be gradually freed from the tiresome business of providing Pleasures as temptations. . . . As habit renders the pleasures of vanity and excitement and flippancy at once less pleasant and harder to forgo (for this is what habit fortunately does to a pleasure) you will find that anything or nothing is sufficient to attract his wandering attention. You no longer need a good book, which he really likes, to keep him from his prayers or his work or his sleep; a column of advertisements in yesterday's paper will do. You can make him waste his time not only in conversation he enjoys with people whom he likes, but in conversations with those he cares nothing about on subjects that bore him. . . . You can keep him up late at night, not roistering, but staring at a dead fire in a cold room. All the healthy and outgoing activities which we want to avoid can be inhibited and *nothing* given in return.[2]

Fear of Advancing Age

In addition to the fact that the titillation first found in any pleasure cannot be sustained, hedonists face another problem: they inevitably grow old. They must cope with the growing awareness that with advancing age our sex drive declines, our hearing and eyesight fail, and rich food and drink have a greater effect on our stomachs, hearts, and livers (12:1–5). "Swingers," both men and women, find their life-style tinged with a sense of urgency as the years pass, and panic begins to set in as the faces around them look younger and younger. The sense of their own mortality adds anxiety to their daily drive to "grab for all the gusto you can."

We must conclude with Solomon that pleasure for its own sake is a meaningless, unrewarding, deceptive goal. Pursuit of physical gratification continuously arouses ever-widening appetites, yet our appetite is never satisfied. As Solomon points out, it is God's plan that *pleasure should instead come as a by-product of proper living.* He writes: "That every man may eat and drink, and find satisfaction in all his toil—this is a gift of God" (3:13).

God wants us to have our senses, which He created, satisfied with every good thing from His hand (James 1:17). But only He can show us how to do this in a godly manner. Only He can give us pleasure that increases, rather than fades, with the passing of time. When we come and learn from Him, the Creator of all appetite and every thing that delights, we will say with the psalmist, "You have made known to me the path of life; you will fill me with joy in your presence, with eternal pleasures at your right hand" (Ps. 16:11).

* * * *

FINDING THE MEANING

1. Look up *hedonism* in a dictionary. What does it mean? How long do you think the hedonistic philosophy has been popular? _____

   _____

   _____

2. Try to find some information about life during the last days of the Roman Empire. How did they express their hedonistic philosophy? _____

_____

_____

3. What happens when people satisfy their urges outside of God's plan? (See Romans 1:21–32.) What happened to Rome, the recipient of this letter from Paul?

_____

_____

4. What hedonistic tendencies do you see in our culture?

_____

_____

5. Why are hedonistic pursuits "chasing after the wind"?

_____

6. Does God know how to satisfy the human heart? (See Psalm 23; 107:9). What other Scriptures can you find to support your answer? _____

_____

_____

7. What warning does God give to hedonists in Israel? (See Isaiah 5:11–15.) How could we apply this to our nation?

_____

_____

8. Which of Jesus' temptations apply to this lesson? (See Matthew 4:1–11.) How did He combat temptation?

_____

_____

_____

9. Is there some area of life in which you are pursuing pleasure apart from the will of God? What should you do about it? (See Isaiah 55:7) _____

_____

_____

10. How do Isaiah 55:1–3, John 4:13, and John 6:35 relate to this chapter? _____

_____

_____

_____

11. Why, do you think, people hide deep hurts behind a façade of laughter? _____

_____

_____

12. What is the trouble with pleasure? _____

_____

_____

3

THE TROUBLE WITH POSSESSIONS

Ecclesiastes 2:4–11; 5:10–20

Closely related to the pursuit of pleasure is the philosophy of materialism, for we find that in seeking pleasure "under the sun" we inevitably seem to gather more and more things. We need a television set in order to entertain ourselves, and later, perhaps, the additional expense of a hookup to cable TV, or a videotape to catch programs we missed. We must have a stereo, of course, for otherwise how can we hear pleasing music? And, naturally, we need to buy a new record or tape now and then! We start a hobby out of simple interest, but find that we can advance only so far in it without purchasing additional equipment.

Even an enjoyment of the beauties of nature can seem to demand acquiring an atonishing amount of paraphernalia: picnic baskets, fishing gear, camping equipment, cameras and lenses, vans, trailers, motorhomes, and boats. Every sport has its requirements: shoes, rackets, balls, bats, clubs, cycles, special clothing, and of course fields, waterways, pools, courts, and gymnasiums.

In Solomon's day, as in every other age, people naturally turned to materialism in their search for something to lighten the strains of living. They surrounded themselves with as much beauty as they could find, as much luxury and comfort as they could afford, and amassed as much wealth and as many possessions as possible. "I undertook great projects," says Solomon. "I built houses for myself and planted vineyards. I made gardens and parks and planted all kinds of fruit trees in them. I made reservoirs to water groves of flourishing trees" (vv. 4–5).

More and more often in our society both husband and wife must be employed in order to afford to live in places that seem to promise a better life for ourselves and our children. Of course, a new home, or an old one for that matter, cannot just sit there on a patch of dirt. Our enjoyment and self-respect (and possibly a homeowners' agreement that accompanied the sale) require that the ground be covered with grass, shrubs and trees, and perhaps even fountains, patios, and brickwork. Few have the patience to plant seeds and wait months or years for lawn and plants to mature. More often, we rely on instant landscaping of our homes and businesses, using sod, six-foot trees, and five-gallon shrubs.

When Solomon referred to his foray into house building as a great project, he was not making an idle comment. In 1 Kings 7:1–12 we find that his Palace of the Forest of Lebanon took thirteen years to complete. With its columns, courtyard, colonnade, portico, throne hall, Hall of Justice, and spacious living quarters for him and his wife, all made of "high-grade stones, cut to size, and cedar beams," it ought to have satisfied any human being's desire for beauty, comfort, and elegant living.

Of course, such extensive holdings demanded great expenditures. As any homeowner knows, bigger estates require more—and more lavish—furnishings. Empty rooms must be filled with sofas, tables, chairs, beds, lamps, pictures, and knickknacks. In addition, in order to keep house, we need our stoves, refrigerators, vacuum cleaners, lawn mowers, outdoor furniture, dishwashers, microwave ovens, and a hundred other items, all of which must be replaced or repaired at times. Solomon, too, had labor-saving devices, slaves, to keep things tidy (v. 7), and they were an expense to him, much as our appliances are to us.

Solomon did not have electronic means to pipe music throughout the palace, but he did have men and women singers (v. 8) to add relaxing atmosphere to his surroundings. In addition, he says, "I also owned more herds and flocks than anyone in Jerusalem before me. I amassed silver and gold for myself, and the treasure of kings and provinces" (2:7–8). If we read the details of Solomon's lifestyle in 1 Kings 10:14–29, we see that from the twenty-five tons of gold he received yearly to the latest-model chariot, Solomon knew how to live well. Here was a man who surely could enjoy life completely.

But what is Solomon's testimony? "Yet when I surveyed all that my hands had done and what I had toiled to achieve, everything was meaningless, a chasing after the wind; nothing was gained under the sun" (2:11). Does he really mean it, or is he just trying to sound religious? Does he actually remain unfulfilled in spite of all his wonderful possessions and accomplishments? After all, he says "Money is the answer for everything" (10:19).

Limits of Possessions

But Solomon does not really believe this last statement. For in Ecclesiastes 5:10–20 he outlines the limits of possessions as a life goal and warns against the god of materialism. In verse 10 he says, "Whoever loves money never has money enough; whoever loves wealth is never satisfied with his income." A wealthy financier was once asked, "How much money does a person actually need?" He answered, "Always a little bit more." The moment we have one desire gratified, we immediately begin looking around for something else. What happens to the long-awaited pay raise, the tax refund, the unexpected windfall? "As goods increase, so do those who consume them," Solomon observes (v. 11).

Not only does money seem to vanish into thin air, but wealth brings problems of its own. "The abundance of the rich man permits him no sleep" (v. 12), as he worries about investments, deals, and cash flow. If a person tries to hoard wealth, he or she can bring on harm, or have a misfortune and lose everything (v. 14). As Jesus warned, moth, rust, and thieves can do away with any earthly treasure (Matt. 6:19). If our happiness depends on this, we are at the mercy of natural disasters, financial reverses, and changing styles.

Think for a moment. Do the things you bought last year satisfy you today? Will you ever come to the place where you won't want to acquire anything more? Do you feel that urge to buy a car every time the new models are introduced? Are you content with your carpet, or are you eyeing a newer weave? Does this season's dress length cause you to feel the need for a more fashionable wardrobe? Is there a dishwasher that cleans better or rusts slower than the one you have?

Materialism is a hard taskmaster, demanding more and more toil and yielding less and less satisfaction and much pain. We start out thrilled and excited over every new item we obtain. But when the bills come in and debts pile up, the fun fades. We begin to realize we will never be able to afford all the things we see others enjoying, and frustration and discontent arise. Even Solomon, who had everything that was available in his day, found that "as a man comes, so he departs, and what does he gain since he toils for the wind? All his days he eats in darkness, with great frustration, affliction, and anger" (vv. 16–17).

Just as Satan promises satisfaction in the pursuit of pleasure, so he assures us that fulfillment will come as we acquire more material wealth. Instead, we learn from experience that materialism has less attractive offspring: frustration, discontent, anger, self-pity, greed, envy, and ingratitude, to name a few. We also find that, like pleasure, the pursuit of possessions leads us away from God. Demas, we read, left his ministry with Paul "because he loved this world" (2 Tim. 4:10). Many people today have no place of real Christian service because all their time and energy is consumed by their preoccupation with "the good life" or the extra jobs they take in order to keep up with the lifestyle of some social set.

We should believe the Bible rather than the misleading, profit-conscious advertisements in print and on the airwaves as we consider the promises regarding possessions. A watchband will not bring us love; a car will not guarantee success with the opposite sex; a brand name of stockings will not render us irresistible. The devil lies, Jesus said (John 8:44), but the Word of God is true (John 17:17), and it warns:

> People who want to get rich fall into temptation and a trap and into many foolish and harmful desires that plunge men into ruin and destruction. For the love of money is a root of all kinds of evil. Some people, eager for money, have wandered from the faith and pierced themselves with many griefs (1 Tim. 6:9–10).
>
> A greedy man brings trouble to his family (Prov. 15:27).
>
> A faithful man will be richly blessed, but one eager to get rich will not go unpunished (Prov. 28:20).

These are sobering words. An insatiable desire to lead an ever more luxurious and glamorous life is *not* a minor matter, it is deadly sin. Greed is sin. Envy is sin. Ingratitude to God for what He has given us is sin. When we covet anything belonging to someone else, we are breaking the tenth commandment (Exod. 20:17). As we chase the bubbles of fulfillment through possessions, we will find them bursting in our hands even as they draw us farther and farther down the path away from God. Jesus warns, "Watch out! Be on your guard against all kinds of greed; a man's life does not consist in the abundance of his possessions" (Luke 12:15).

Facing Up to Greed

We can keep the sins of envy, greed, and covetousness hidden from ourselves and others most of the time. We can put on a gracious and spiritually deceptive exterior and cover up the rapacious discontent gnawing away on the inside. But the woman whose desire for things is not under God's control will reveal her inner warfare by nagging her husband, by making bitter comments to friends, by spending hours reading advertisements or window shopping, or by her inability to keep her spending within the limits of her income.

Jesus said that money and what it represents is actually a rival for our worship of the true God. He taught, "No one can serve two masters. Either he will hate the one and love the other, or he will be devoted to the one and despise the other. You cannot serve both God and Money" (Matt. 6:24).

One quick way to tell who is winning the battle for first place in your life is by considering your response to God's standard of giving Him 10 percent of your income. Your attitude toward tithing will reveal what really masters your heart. Giving a tenth of our earnings to the Lord is a repeated command in Scripture (Lev. 27:30, 32; Mal. 3:10), and is acknowledged by Jesus as expected behavior for God's people (Matt. 23:23). God even says that we are robbing Him if we do not bring our tithes and offerings to Him (Mal.

3:8–10). But the thought of giving so much to the Lord often causes people to panic, for they realize that if they do so it means that they will not be able to afford some of the things they had their hearts set on, or for which they have already run up bills.

The call to tithing brings our tendency toward greed, ingratitude, and materialism out of the realm of rationalization and into the open. We may be able to convince ourselves that we are not *really* covetous or grasping, but merely enjoying beauty. We may argue that our negative attitude does not stem from discontent with the life God has given us. But we cannot talk our way around the act of tithing: we either do it or we don't.

Tithing will not ensure that greed will never be a problem to us (we can even begrudge our giving), but it will be a tangible indication as to who our true Master is, and prove our determination to keep our desires under control. It will also help us to enjoy what we are able to buy with the rest of our income.

Following God's Priorities

Solomon agrees that we can only enjoy the possessions we have when we know we are following God's plan for us and when our priorities are correct: "Moreover, when God gives any man wealth and possessions, and enables him to enjoy them, to accept his lot and be happy in his work—this is a gift of God" (Eccl. 5:19). Those who get their wealth by unfair means will not be happy (Prov. 20:17, 23). Those who get more money to spend by cheating on their income tax will not have God's blessing (Matt. 22:15–22). Any who do not "seek God first" by giving Him His rightful 10 percent of their income have their priorities wrong and will find the other 90 percent slipping through their fingers as well (Prov. 23:4–5).

Past, Present, Future

Besides, what happens to all the possessions we work and scheme to acquire? Solomon says, "I hated all the things I had toiled for under the sun, because I must leave them to the one who comes after me. And who knows whether he will be a wise man or a fool? Yet he will have control over all the work into which I have poured my effort and skill under the sun" (2:18–19). Something treasured by us may mean nothing to our heirs and be given to charity. Our beloved home may be sold to someone who uproots the trees and lawn and puts in cement and ornamental rock.

The god of materialism offers nothing permanent to the woman who succumbs to it. She does not view the past with satisfaction because she never got all she wanted. The present is unappreciated because her whole focus is on the next paycheck, on a future shopping spree, or on her or her husband's desired promotion. How much better is the lot of the woman who trusts in God. She can regard the past as part of God's plan for her life. She can enjoy her family, her home, her entire life now because she knows God will add to her everything He wants her to have (Matt. 6:33). The passing of years does not disturb the trusting person, "for he will not often consider the years of his life, because God keeps him occupied with the gladness of his heart" (Eccl. 5:20 NASB).

Job was a man forced to come to grips with both having and losing great possesssions. His faith is echoed by Solomon in Ecclesiastes, "Naked a man comes from his mother's womb, and as he comes, so he departs. He takes nothing from his labor that he can carry in his hand" (5:15). If we cannot affirm with Job that it is the Lord who gives and the Lord who takes away and still say, "May the name of the LORD be praised" (Job 1:21), we are not prepared for the demands life places on us.

We cannot "take it with us," and we cannot control what

our heirs do with what we leave them. As we consider our possessions, it seems wise to make God's view, from His perspective "above the sun," our view. For that will not only ease our emotions and increase our peace now, but it will be the view we will live with for eternity.

* * * *

FINDING THE MEANING

1. Look up *materialism* in a dictionary. What does it mean? When do you think materialism began? _____

_____

_____

2. Read Matthew 6:25–34. What can be said about those who worry about money and possessions? _____

_____

_____

_____

3. How does the parable in Luke 12:13–21 relate to our study? _____

_____

_____

_____

4. Are you guilty of the sin of greed? What should you do? (See 1 John 1:9) _____

_____

_____

_____

5. Can you say with certainty that God gave you your possessions (5:19), or did you get them by means unapproved by God? _____

_____

6. What is promised to those who give God His tithe? (See Malachi 3:8–11.) Do you believe this promise?

_____

7. How do possessions relate to the warning in 1 John 2:16 (NASB) against "the lust of the flesh and the lust of the eyes and the boastful pride of life"? _____

_____

_____

8. What is your view of yourself? Does your self-image in fact consist in what Luke 12:15 calls "the abundance of [your] possessions"? _____

_____

_____

9. If it seems that all your efforts and accomplishments are meaningless, what can you do? (See Proverbs 3:5–6; 16:3; 1 Peter 5:7.) _____

_____

10. What do you think Solomon would say to a mother considering employment outside her home? _____

_____

_____

11. What is the trouble with possessions? _____

_____

_____

4

THE TROUBLE WITH WISDOM

Ecclesiastes 2:12–26; 3:1–8; 9:13–10:4

Having ruled out pleasure and possessions as goals that will bring humans true fulfillment, Solomon says, "I turned my thoughts to consider wisdom, and also madness and folly" (2:12). Since Solomon had a life-long interest in wisdom—"I have grown and increased in wisdom more than anyone who has ruled over Jerusalem before me; I have experienced much of wisdom and knowledge" (1:16)—it is surprising that he did not turn to wisdom first. But Solomon knew that the average person does not consider first mental pursuits, but physical comforts; it is only when our physical needs have been met that we are willing to engage in contemplation. People rarely consider knowledge as a way of finding meaning in life until other pursuits have proven futile.

God's Wisdom Vs. Human Wisdom

Solomon, though experienced in the kind of wisdom that comes as a gift from God, must now try to explore human wisdom and its related areas, madness and folly. He only finds, however, "that this, too, is a chasing after wind" (1:17). The reason for this is that the more aware we are, the more we see the bad as well as the good. When our consciousness is raised, we begin to recognize more problems. "For with much wisdom comes much sorrow; the more knowledge, the more grief" (1:18). Human wisdom raises many questions, but finds few answers.

God's wisdom is "first pure; then peace loving, considerate, submissive, full of mercy and good fruit, impartial and sincere" (James 3:17). In contrast, the Bible says that our wisdom in our natural state is "earthly, unspiritual, of the devil" (James 3:15). Our intellect was tainted on the day Eve and Adam decided to acquire wisdom Satan's way instead of God's way. "When the woman saw that the fruit of the tree was . . . desirable for gaining wisdom, she took some and ate it" (Gen. 3:6).

Intellectualism's Fatal Flaw

This is intellectualism's fatal flaw: its validity rests entirely on the reliability of our reasoning power. But "what is twisted cannot be straightened; what is lacking cannot be counted" (1:15). Water can rise only to its own level; inferior musical instruments emit inferior tones; a fallen intellect produces faulty conclusions.

For example, consider the efforts of women and men down through the ages to explain and worship a supernatural being according to their own best insights. The resulting religions have spawned such things as idol worship, human sacrifice, animism, reincarnation, mutilation, temple prostitution, drug-induced states, and occultism. Some brilliant minds deny the possibility of any supernatural dimension at all. Despite the fact that God says that His "eternal power and divine nature have been clearly seen, being understood from what has been made, so that men are without excuse" (Rom. 1:20), our intellect has been unable to discern it correctly on its own. When the Bible says, "The fear of the LORD is the beginning of wisdom, and knowledge of the Holy One is understanding" (Prov. 9:10), it is making it clear that those who discount God have not even taken the first step toward real success in intellectual matters.

Wisdom's Uses

We have, however, been somewhat successful in applying our wisdom to earthly matters. From experience we have learned that "wisdom is better than folly, just as light is better than darkness" (2:13), and that "wisdom brightens a man's face and changes its hard appearance" (8:1). We have found that people who act prudently, who live wisely, come to less harm and generally live longer (7:11–12). Some people may even discover, through trial and error (their own or others'), "the stupidity of wickedness and the madness of folly" (7:25). Wise individuals have even been known to outsmart entire armies, proving that wisdom is better than strength (9:13–16), or weapons of war (9:18).

The intellectual also can gain from observation a rational view of human existence. Such people can suspend their emotions and conclude that there is, on the whole, "a time for everything and a season for every activity under heaven" (3:1–8). One need not be disturbed because something is torn, for that is to be expected—there will be a time to mend. There is a time to scatter and to gather, to weep and to laugh, to kill and to heal. This philosophy can be a comfort in times of stress, and such a sensible and dispassionate view can keep a person from either becoming overborn by the trials of life or unduly elated in prosperity.

The Limits of Wisdom

Wisdom does have its limits, however. Though "wisdom is better than strength," it is apparently no match for foolishness. By stating that "one sinner destroys much good" (9:18), and saying that "as dead flies give perfume a bad smell, so a little folly outweighs wisdom and honor" (10:1), Solomon seems to have concluded that one bad apple of foolishness can spoil a whole barrelful of wisdom.

It is not unusual to hear someone bemoaning the trouble caused by the stupidity of another, but in fact even our intellect cannot keep us from acting foolishly at times. How many of us live up to our own best insights? Our emotions, our inner needs of various kinds often cause us to act imprudently. We know we haven't enough money to buy both a particular dress and our week's groceries, but we purchase the outfit anyway. A doctor tells his patients to give up cigarettes but smokes two packs a day himself. A mother forbids her children to eat before dinner but snacks the whole time she is preparing the meal.

Intelligent people take risks all the time, and even sometimes bring ruin to themselves and their families, blotting out of their minds the possible disastrous consequences, and gambling on the chance that everything will work out. Stunt men are not dumb. It takes brains to play the stock market. Con men have to be both smart and personable to succeed.

Intelligence, by itself, is no guarantee that a person will live on a higher plane than others less endowed or handle temptations more wisely. When the successful businessman in the movie *Plaza Suite* confessed to his wife that he had been having an affair with his secretary, his wife cried, "Your secretary! *Anyone* can have an affair with his *secretary!* I had expected better from you than that!" Very able people become involved in the most common, unimaginative sins, because their emotions and impulses are not under control any more than an average person's.

Intellectualism has other drawbacks as a philosophy, for it is of little help when dealing with the big questions of life and death. The wise may avoid, through a rational approach, some of the pitfalls of living that the foolish person does not, but in the end "the same fate overtakes them both" (2:14). The wise person may well ask, "What then do I gain by being wise?" (2:15), for "the wise man too must die" (2:16).

Not only that, but wise people are not remembered any longer that the foolish; both will be forgotten (2:16; 9:15). And, adding insult to injury, when a wise person dies, some fool may receive the benefit of all he has amassed or all she has established with wisdom, knowledge, and skill (2:21). All his days he worked with anxious striving, even at night her intellect kept going, and what does this person get for it? Pain, grief, and oblivion. "This too is meaningless and a great misfortune" (2:21).

Human Wisdom Cannot Tell Why

So those set on discovering the deep meanings of life through an intellectual approach remain confused. They can gather the pieces of the puzzle, but they cannot see how they fit together. They can often answer the question "What?" but not "Why?" When they try to probe beyond their own experience or that of others, they can only speculate; without divine revelation they cannot know. They can hypothesize, but in the end they must confess with Solomon, "This was beyond me. Whatever wisdom may be, it is far off and most profound—who can discover it?" (7:23–24). "No one can comprehend what goes on under the sun. Despite all his efforts to search it out, man cannot discover its meaning. Even if a wise man claims he knows, he cannot really comprehend it" (8:17).

God's Wisdom: Jesus Christ

The inability of philosophers to make sense out of what happens on earth is not caused by a failure to exercise their full mental capacities, it is a limitation placed upon us by God. Our human existence can never be explained apart from the spiritual dimension, and God does not allow the "natural man" to pierce the veil surrounding such knowledge. The wisdom of God seems foolishness to people in their unregenerate state, when in fact "the foolishness of God is wiser than men." The most basic areas of life—for example, how one can know about God and His workings with women and men made in His image—cannot be discovered without divine help. In fact, we cannot understand spiritual matters without receiving Jesus Christ, who *is* both "the power of God and the wisdom of God."

> Where is the wise man? Where is the scholar? Where is the philosopher of this age? Has not God made foolish the wisdom of the world? For since in the wisdom of God the world through its wisdom did not know him, God was pleased through the foolishness of what was preached to save those who believe. Jews demand miraculous signs and Greeks look for wisdom, but we preach Christ crucified; a stumbling block to Jews and foolishness to Gentiles, but to those whom God has called, both Jews and Greeks, Christ the power of God and the wisdom of God. For the foolishness of God is wiser than man's wisdom, and the weakness of God is stronger than man's strength (1 Cor. 1:20–25).

Jesus spent much of His ministry teaching people God's wisdom. At the end of the Sermon on the Mount (Matt. 5–7), He said that those who would be wise must not only hear His words, but *do* them. They would be like a man who built his house on the rock where it could withstand the worst storms of life. He said the person who heard His words and did *not* act on them was like a foolish man who built his house on the sand. When the same calamities struck that house, it fell. Earthly philosophers who do not turn to Jesus Christ as the Way, the Truth, and the Life (John 14:6) are judged foolish by God and are condemned to failure of the most eternal kind, no matter what brilliant propositions they may pose. Women who want to have safe homes must build them, not on what the world says, but on Jesus' words.

God's Wisdom Adds Joy

In the preceding chapters we found that only God can give us the gift of satisfaction with our lives, that to be happy with our possessions, our work, our bodies, was impossible apart from the Lord. Now, after concluding that on our own we cannot comprehend the meaning of life, Solomon affirms, "To the man who pleases him, God gives wisdom, knowledge and happiness" (2:26). This is the only time Solomon links happiness with wisdom. Earthly wisdom applied to daily activities may ease our mortal life and keep us from some painful mistakes, but it does not bring lasting delight (1:18). Only God can give the heavenly wisdom that brings joy. Our minds, as well as our spirits and our bodies, are dependent on Him for fulfillment.

Solomon's enjoyment of wisdom came only when he was using godly insight rather than straining his human intellect. What earthbound minds can never discover, God delights in revealing. He is the One who sees beyond death, and it is He who tells us what goes on outside the limits of time and space where we cannot see so that we can interpret correctly what we can see (1 Cor. 2:8–9). Even then we are limited by our own powers of understanding. "He has also set eternity in the hearts of men; yet they cannot fathom what God has done from beginning to end" (Eccl. 3:11).

It is surely madness and folly to try to make decisions on

our own, when godly insight is ours for the asking. We begin to be wise when we decide to take God up on His promise, "If any of you lacks wisdom, he should ask God, who gives generously to all without finding fault, and it will be given to him" (James 1:5).

* * * *

FINDING THE MEANING

1. Look up *intellectualism* and *rationalism* in a dictionary. What do they mean? _____

_____

_____

2. Read Proverbs 8. What are some advantages of obtaining wisdom? What use did the Lord make of God's wisdom?

_____

_____

_____

3. How could Ecclesiastes 11:1–2 typify a rational approach to life? _____

_____

4. What was Eve's purpose in wanting to become wise? (See Genesis 3:5.) _____

_____

5. What was the immediate result of Eve's gaining knowledge of good and evil? (See Genesis 3:10.) _____

_____

_____

6. Where can we find God's wisdom today? (See Psalm 19:7; 2 Timothy 3:15–17.) _____

_____

_____

7. How does Jeremiah 9:23–24 summarize our study in Ecclesiastes so far? _____

_____

_____

8. Do you have God's Wisdom, Jesus Christ, in your life? How can you obtain Him? (See John 1:12.) _____

_____

_____

9. Which aspect of God's wisdom in James 3:17 is most lacking in your life? What can you do about it? (See James 4:7.) _____

_____

_____

10. Can you cite some instances when you have acted contrary to your best insight? What does this show? _____

_____

_____

11. What is the trouble with intellectualism? _____

_____

_____

5

THE TROUBLE WITH EVOLUTION

Ecclesiastes 3:18–22

"There are one hundred and ninety-three living species of monkeys and apes. One hundred and ninety-two of them are covered with hair. The exception is a naked ape self-named *Homo sapiens*." With these words Desmond Morris began his best-selling book entitled *The Naked Ape: A Zoologist's Study of the Human Animal.*[1] Although the human has behavior patterns that are "rather complex and impressive," and has acquired "lofty new motives," Morris concludes that he is "an ape nevertheless." Relentlessly referring to "the male of the species" or "the female of the species" throughout the book, he considers such topics as origins, sex, rearing, exploration, feeding, and comfort as a zoologist would treat them from the observation of a group of animals!

If we are repulsed by such a low view of human existence, we should realize that it is but a natural extension of the atheistic theories of human origins that have become the accepted view throughout the scientific community and in our public schools in recent years. If the supernatural dimension is discounted, if we are confined to what we can deduce by ourselves from the world around us, a logical conclusion is that we have no higher beginning or ultimate purpose than do the animals with whom we share the earth.

Solomon, writing from the perspective of unaided human wisdom as he discusses the problem of the origin and destiny of animal and human life, struggles with the same thoughts:

> I also thought, "As for men, God tests them so that they may see that they are like animals. Man's fate is like that of the animals; the same fate awaits them both: As one dies, so dies the other. All have the same breath; man has no advantage over the animal. Everything is meaningless. All go to the same place; all come from dust, and to dust all return" (3:18–20).

Evolution and Creation: Both Impossible to Prove

Despite all our study, including continuous excavation, cataloging fossil records, analysis of genetic changes, and rock dating, scientists realize that the theory of evolution can never be proved. Neither can creationists prove their contentions scientifically, for no one can live long enough to conduct the kinds of experiments necessary to prove or disprove either theory. Evolutionists cannot wait the millions of years they believe it takes for one species to evolve, and creationists obviously cannot travel back through time to observe their beginnings.

But we *can* observe the kinds of attitude and behavior that naturally follow upon a person's convictions regarding the origins of the universe and its inhabitants, convictions based on faith rather than proof. There is either an absolute standard for moral behavior or there is not. There is either a mighty, intelligent Power to whom we are responsible, or we are answerable to ourselves and our fellow creatures alone. A woman who believes she will be held accountable by God will behave far differently than the woman who believes she will not be judged for her actions by any deity.

Animals Are Not Responsible for Their Actions

The moral decline of our nation is still being retarded somewhat by the Judeo-Christian ethic that gave it its birth, its law, and its moral foundation. Around the world, peoples who retain vestiges of the worship of the true God place at least some restraint on the moral decay of their nations, while cultures immersed in atheism or worship of evil spirits display the barbarism common to other primates (Rom. 3:10–18).

Of course, if we accept the notion that we are only animals, there is no logical reason for us to act in a manner different from other members of the animal kingdom. A mother fish who eats her young, a mother dog who pushes an unwanted puppy away from its only source of food and survival, are simply acting in response to some innate impulse. A black widow spider poisons the male after mating and leaves her eggs in his body to hatch. Later she devours him. Some species of animals mate indiscriminately during their mating season. Cuckoos push the defenseless young of other kinds of birds over the sides of their nests to their deaths, and lay their own eggs there. With some primates, the males fight until one dies, the winner taking a particular female as the prize.

For animals the basic drives for survival, reproduction, and in some cases territory, are all that matter. No moral judgment is appropriate on activities controlled by animal instinct: If humans are merely animals, they cannot be held responsible for their actions.

If we are but another species of animal, all our actions must be reinterpreted. Marriage is not a permanent relationship ordained by God and subject to His rules governing it (Gen. 2:24; Mal. 2:14–16; Eph. 5:22–28). It is instead an evolved expression of the pair-formation of hunting animals in which the male seeks to ensure the fidelity of the female while he is hunting for food.[2] Smiling in a baby is its way of attaching the mother emotionally to it and pacifying her, and in the adult smiling is a "grooming-invitation" signal, a substitute for the lip-smacking of the monkey.[3] Talking is a somewhat more complex form of the inborn mammalian repertoire of grunts and squeals, since the tone of voice often conveys the meaning without even thinking about the content of the words.[4] Medical practice has evolved out of social grooming behavior (picking foreign objects out of each other's fur) of chimpanzees and is now the major expression of our animal comfort behavior,[5] and so on.

Facing the Implications Honestly

Christians who accept evolutionary theory are trying to have the best of both worlds: they want to remain in the mainstream of current scientific thought, but at the same time want to hold that we have transcended our roots and somehow shed our baser nature along the way—though why it is base for an animal merely to express its instincts is not clear. Morris is at least being honest when he forces us to face the inescapable truth that if we are evolved animals we are not going to understand ourselves correctly or be fulfilled while we continue to recoil at accepting that fact. He maintains that "in acquiring lofty new motives, he has lost none of the early old ones. . . . His old impulses have been with him for millions of years, his new ones only a few thousand years at most—and there is no hope of quickly shrugging off the accumulated genetic legacy of his whole evolutionary past."[6]

The Limits of Education

It has been popular in this century to believe that education is the answer to the ills of humankind. Ignoring the lessons of past highly cultured but cruel civilizations, some are con- vinced that if we instill in our evolved brains enough philosophy, music, art, literature, and similar elevated disci- plines, we will civilize our base impulses and live on a higher plane than that of the lower animals. The fact that we have at times acted in a charitable, moral, or enlightened manner has led some to believe that education has been successful. How- ever, even Morris asserts that training and modification can- not develop new traditions. Changes of marked degree in actions must be genetic changes, he claims.[7]

The person of faith agrees that genetic changes are required—special creation, in fact. When God created man as a completely new kind of being in His own image, the earth for the first time contained a creature with a spiritual nature. It is because of this unique spiritual nature that we can, unlike other creatures, transcend our physical nature. It is not, then, cultural education, but religious education that teaches people to distinguish between right and wrong, to deny themselves for the sake of others, to act to ensure justice rather than encourage lawlessness. Down through the cen- turies, it has been our awareness of the requirements of a loving, holy, and just God that has moved us to act in other than our own selfish interests (Gal. 5:17–24; Phil. 2:1–8). Even individuals who deny the existence of God have nevertheless had to conform to biblically inspired standards of behavior in Western civilizations if they desired the ap- proval of their fellow humans.

If we are only animals, then those who look to secular education as our salvation are being totally illogical, for ani- mals can be expected to revert to untamed behavior without warning no matter what their training. The most domesticated lion or boa constrictor cannot be trusted to remain harmless; some have turned on loving masters for no apparent reason. The fact that brilliant men have committed unspeakable acts shows that education by itself does not affect human behavior permanently unless a spiritual commitment is made and outside spiritual power is obtained (Rom. 7:18–25; 8:9). If lasting change is to be effected, human beings can and must be approached on that spiritual level that is not present in any other living creature.

The Evolution of Humanism

Those who dismiss the idea of any supernatural dimension and view man as the highest form of life to have yet evolved are left with only humans to admire and esteem. From this circumstance modern humanism has sprung. Classical humanism did not consider itself in conflict with Christian beliefs, but primarily sought to emphasize the dignity and freedom of man and promote the study of the humanities as opposed to science. Secular humanism, however, rejects the idea of God and proclaims, "No deity will save us, we must save ourselves. Promises of immortal salvation are both illusory and harmful."[8] As one writer explains:

> Many philosophers in the past have argued that man's deep-rooted craving for a God and for an intelligible world are clear indications that a rational deity must exist . . . since the universe does not make sense in human terms, there must be a suprarational Being to explain it. The humanists will have none of this.[9]

The Sins That Spring from Humanism

God does not view this kind of thinking as understandable or excusable error but as willful rejection of the evidence of His invisible attributes, especially His eternal power and divine nature, which He claims even unrighteous people can see in the world around them. God insists that those who do not recognize Him as God are in their wickedness purposefully suppressing the truth, and that they will experience His wrath because of it (Rom. 1:18–20). Secular humanists have "exchanged the glory of the incorruptible God for an image in the form of corruptible man. . . . For they exchanged the truth of God for a lie, and worshiped and served the creature rather than the Creator" (Rom. 1:23, 25 NASB).

The section of Scripture immediately following these words makes clear the cause-and-effect relationship between belief and practice. The Bible warns that man-centered philosophies result in a downward spiral into the grossest sins. When man persists in pledging allegiance to himself rather than to God, God "gives him over to shameful lusts": homosexual acts by men and women, depraved minds, every kind of evil, greed and depravity, murder, strife, deceit, disobedience to parents, slander, faithlessness, insolence, ruthlessness, and even more (Rom. 1:26–31). It is no accident that the organizations embracing the humanistic dogma actively endorse and promote homosexuality, abortion, and civil disobedience in the name of human freedom and liberation. Their actions are a logical extension of their godless beliefs.

Humanists, of course, do not view such activities in the same light as Christians do. They do not believe that homosexuality, sexual promiscuity, or abortion are necessarily bad for an individual or for society as a whole; instead *they judge those who hold biblical views as a threat to our free society.* In *The Humanist* magazine, writers Prescott and Wallace assert that people who oppose abortion are not really interested in the life of the fetus—they are simply using that argument to mask the fact that what they really want is to prevent people from enjoying sex.

> The emphasis upon the "reproductive" aspect of sexuality by the anti-abortion movement serves to obscure the central and real issue in the abortion controversy, namely, that the

primary function of human sexuality is for the experiencing and mutual sharing of sexual pleasure. It is this primacy of physical pleasure in the human sexual relationship that cannot be accepted by the anti-abortionist mentality.[10]

The writers also obtained the voting records of the members of the Pennsylvania senate on three bills: one making fornication and adultery a summary offense (1973), one limiting the use of public money to pay for abortions for only those mothers whose lives were endangered (1977), and one forbidding governmental agencies from hiring homosexuals or convicted or admitted sex offenders for a specified list of positions. Then they compared these records with data derived from their own questionnaire given to "a variety of individuals and groups" (primarily college audiences and drug rehabilitation groups) and further concluded:

> The anti-abortion mentality is characterized by authoritarian control of individuals; a high value on physical pain, punishment and violence; and the most significant correlates are those of punitive and repressive attitudes toward sexual expressiveness and pleasure. In short, it is the personality profile of the neo-fascist.[11]

Humanism Cannot Realize Its Own Goals

If in the name of human dignity, freedom, and worth, humanists defend behavior that can only degrade the human personality, it is not necessarily because they intend to do so. Their writings call for the growth of many of the same values that Christians desire. They honor truth and beauty (although our definitions might differ), and commend kindness in human dealings. But they are at a loss as to how to make people moral.

In an article promisingly entitled *The Makings of a Good Person*, Joan Share, a psychological counselor, deplores the poor character seen in all humans but most blatantly expressed by children, and lists such negative traits as brutality, insensitivity, sadism, self-centeredness, power struggles, bragging, and humiliating others. However, she criticizes those who look to religious institutions for help in character building: "Religious schools don't usually endeavor to pursue this [the teaching of morality] beyond teaching perfunctory memorization of the Ten Commandments with the same gusto as memorizing dates for a social studies quiz." She asserts, without any substantiating data, that religious training is "often counter-productive in this realm by its insidious promotion of prejudice and intolerance."[12]

What then does she suggest as a way of teaching "kindness, compassion, love, honesty, tolerance, and individuality"? Admitting that "as a humanist, my cynicism is tempered by an optimism about the potential goodness of human nature," and that "good persons" do not "happen automatically" but "are to some extent molded," Share nevertheless has not one concrete suggestion to propose as to how to accomplish the transformation. She concludes plaintively:

> There are so many possibilities of creative approaches to this idea, only waiting to be instituted by adults who are dedicated to the development of better people and a better society. Somewhere in the overloaded circuits of soccer, tennis, piano lessons, television, and social fanfare there must be a vacant outlet to plug in the teaching of good character.[13]

What Ms. Share does not comprehend is that an "outlet" is only useful if there is a power source behind it. Humanists have cut themselves off from the Source of the power that can tell them not just what to do, but why and how, and can also enable them to become noble people. Jesus said, "You will receive power when the Holy Spirit comes on you" (Acts 1:8).

Hedonistic Attitudes Expected

As Solomon points out, the only sensible thing for animal-man to do is to try to get what enjoyment there is from life, since that is all we know or will ever know (v. 22). If we really do not know "if the spirit of man rises upward and if the spirit of the animal goes down into the earth" (v. 21), we should not be surprised if our search for happiness leads us to try every form of diversion that comes our way. There is no governor on the expression of our bodily appetites if there is nothing beyond this life. We are on a level with animals in satisfying our drives for survival, for sex, and for territory, which can only lead to the dissension, wars, ruthlessness, and depravity pictured in the Romans passage we have considered.

Scientists Are Fallible

Scientists make pronouncements regarding the importance and interpretations of their various discoveries with such authority that we often find ourselves trying to believe two opposite assertions at the same time. We try to make room for the theories of unbelieving evolutionists while holding onto our belief in a Creator-God, without resolving the inconsistencies. We act as if we don't understand that beliefs give birth to actions and that our personal lives will be affected by our convictions, whether true or false ones, just as those of unbelievers are.

Certainly, the fittest *are* usually the ones to survive. Obviously, there *is* some kind of natural selection in nature. In our own day, species *are* becoming extinct without special protection. But within recent years, scientists have found skeletons formerly considered important as genetic links to be frauds, have changed their opinions about the date of the "emergence of man" by millions of years, and have discovered widely diverging ages when measuring by radiometric dating samples taken from the same location.[14] Scientific conclusions are not as conclusive as some would have us believe, and they are subject to change as new data surfaces.

Scripture Is Adamant

No truth in Scripture is asserted more often than the fact that God created the universe as a whole and human beings in particular. God repeatedly points to His status as Creator as the basis for our worship of Him and as proof that He can deliver us from any situation (Exod. 20:1–5; Job 38; 39; 40:1–4; Isa. 42:5–8; 45:11–12, 18). If He is not the Creator, then His main argument for deserving our worship is false, and He is not powerful enough to save anyone. We cannot have it both ways.

If God is not Creator, a great portion of the Bible must be cut out and discarded. The Lord God of Israel insists upon our receiving Him as our Creator Lord in all three of His persons. The Father created (Gen. 1:1), the Son created (John 1:1–3; Col. 1:16–17), and the Holy Spirit created (Gen. 1:2, Ps. 104:30). The Triune God said at the creation of man, "Let *us* make man in *our* image, in *our* likeness" (Gen. 1:26).

The woman of faith has no option but to believe that God created us in His image as He said, that we are much more than animals, in fact that we have been crowned with glory and honor to rule over other creatures (Gen. 1:26; Ps. 8:5–6). We will not end up the same way the animals do, but will face God someday; and whether our eternal souls will experience eternal punishment or eternal life depends upon how we have responded to God's claims to be our Creator Lord (John 5:24–29). With Solomon, Christians must rise above the limited view of earthly thinking and affirm that we do not begin or end as the animals do, but that "the spirit returns to God who gave it" (12:7).

FINDING THE MEANING

1. Look up *humanism* in a dictionary. What is the emphasis of humanism? _____

   _____

   _____

2. What does Psalm 8 say about: a) who made the universe, b) who made human beings, c) the worth of humans, d) our relationship to other creatures? _____

   _____

   _____

   _____

   _____

3. How did Jesus compare man and the animal kingdom? (See Matthew 6:26.) _____

   _____

4. What does Scripture have to say about secular humanists? (See Isaiah 29:16.) _____

   _____

5. What does Psalm 139:13–16 have to say to those who favor abortion on the grounds that a fetus is not a living human? _____

   _____

6. What is God's present relationship to His world? (See Psalm 104: 10–32; Matthew 6:26–30.) _____

   _____

   _____

   _____

7. What does Colossians 1:15–17 have to say about how the universe is held together at this moment? _____

   _____

8. Can you identify areas in your life where you have adopted the views of atheistic scientists or humanists? _

   _____

   _____

9. What Scripture passages speak specifically to your problem areas? _____

   _____

10. Is the God you worship the Creator God of the Bible, or some limited god of your own making? Describe this God (god). _____

    _____

    _____

11. What is the trouble with evolution? _____

    _____

    _____

6

THE TROUBLE WITH EXISTENTIALISM

Ecclesiastes 4:1–3; 7:1–10

For those who feel that their involvement in modern philosophies is a mark of sophistication and daring, it must come as something of a disappointment to find that these same ideas were evaluated and discarded three thousand years ago. Solomon states early in Ecclesiastes that even then the wisdom he was analyzing was not original: "There is nothing new under the sun. Is there anything of which one can say, 'Look! This is something new'? It was here already, long ago; it was here before our time" (1:9–10). Those who view evolutionary theory as an adventure into new frontiers of thought are misleading themselves. Those who shout with the modern existentialists, "There is no meaning in life, no absolute values of right and wrong, existence is absurd!" also find that Solomon has stolen the march on them.

Of all philosophies presented in Ecclesiastes, existentialism is the most incomprehensible to the Christian. This is because

Christianity is based on unchanging standards of good and evil, while existentialism denies the existence of absolutes. Christianity insists on a universe created by a rational Being who is accomplishing His purpose, while existentialism denies the possibility of any suprahuman entity, any rational thought, any purpose in the universe. It is a philosophy born out of despair at the inability of either rationalism or idealism to solve the ills of mankind, and which retreats into irrationality as it centers on the freedom of the individual and his or her feelings. Existentialists do not believe a person's actions are determined by heredity, environment, or childhood experiences. Instead we are completely free to choose any course of action and must take responsibility for our choice. However, since there is no standard of good and evil, since "God is dead," a person's actions are morally neutral and nonintellectual. Feeling is more authentic than reason, problems are solved by "passionate choice" without the necessity of any rational justification for making the choice.[1]

It is a nihilistic view, a philosophy of "nothingness": experience has no reality, value, or meaning of itself, but only that which an individual chooses to assign to it. So Friedrich Nietzsche (1844–1900) could assert, "Everything is permitted." As Solomon has showed us, such sentiments are not new. Nihilism is not "a peculiar feature of the modern world. . . . Nihilism has its origin in the nature of man, not in contingent historical events. In one version or another, it may be found in antiquity at various crucial periods, although not, of course, in the precise form it takes today."[2]

How many times in Ecclesiastes have you found Solomon repeating, "This, too, is meaningless"? This book is the pilgrimage of a man trying to cope in life without God (and therefore without purpose or structure), a journey that repeatedly brings him to the brink of despair. Solomon cries out:

The day of death [is] better than the day of birth. It is better to go to the house of mourning than to go to a house of feasting, for death is the destiny of every man; the living should take this to heart (7:1–2).

And I declared that the dead, who had already died, are happier than the living, who are still alive. But better than both is he who has not yet been (4:2–3).

A sense of dread and a preoccupation with pain and death pervade the lives of those caught in the web of existentialist thought. Nothing they do is "bad," but then they can't do anything "good" either, for neither bad nor good exist. Irrational statements are acceptable: "A good name is better than fine perfume, and the day of death better than the day of birth" (7:1). Life is like a nightmare, like living in a Fun House at an amusement park where mirrors distort images at every turn. "Sorrow is better than laughter, because a sad face is good for the heart. The heart of the wise is in the house of mourning, but the heart of fools is in the house of pleasure" (7:3–4).

Since life is purposeless, hope is dead, and one can never look to the future for joy. A person's natural feelings of anticipation at the start of a new venture are dulled because she looks forward to having it over: "The end of a matter is better than its beginning" (7:8). Memories bring little pleasure, for it is because of our failure in the past to cope with problems that rational thinking was abandoned by the existentialists: "Do not say, 'Why were the old days better than these?' For it is not wise to ask such questions" (7:10).

Why Christians Should Deal With Existentialist Thought

Christians often have little patience with such pessimistic thinking. We do not like to dwell on the false teachings of the world, when truth is so much more worthwhile and helpful. But we would do well to grasp at least some of these concepts, because we are bombarded by existentialist thinking every day, and we will not deal with it effectively if we do not recognize it for what it is.

As Francis Schaeffer states in *Escape From Reason,* "Every generation of Christians has this problem of learning how to speak meaningfully to its own age. It cannot be solved without an understanding of the changing existential situation which it faces. If we are to communicate the Christian faith effectively, therefore, we must know and understand the thought forms of our own generation."[3]

How Ordinary People Are Affected

Ordinary people may think that they and their neighbors are not affected by such esoteric brain twisting as existentialist thought appears to be, but they are. People who live on the basis of rational thinking and with a standard of right and wrong attend movies and plays and wonder why they aren't dazzled, as the critics were. They go to an art exhibit and come out saying, "My three-year-old must be a genius." They think they have missed the message, and in a sense they have, because they have not understood that the message is, "There is no message."

A film you are watching does not build to any conclusion and leaves you wondering what it was all about, because that is what the film was saying: "Life is not about anything in particular; it is not going anywhere." You search the entertainment section of your newspaper for some place to go on an evening out, but decide to stay home and do the mending because "those shows always leave me feeling so depressed." Exactly. You are *supposed* to feel depressed. The point of many of the movies is that life is hopeless.

We are influenced by the continuous onslaught of irrational propaganda whether we realize it or not. We begin to think that our black-and-white view of good and evil is harsh, out-moded, extreme. We start agreeing with people who argue, "If it feels good, it can't be wrong." We decide issues on the basis of sympathy for the human predicament instead of on the Word of God. We are tempted to think that world events are careening out of control and that God has forgotten us. Ideas of total freedom for every individual sound good to us and we feel hesitant to enforce any restrictions on personal liberty in any area of life.

Existentialist Beliefs Are False

Each of the sentiments in the preceding paragraph are existentialistic and are counter to the law of God. God's absolute standards are not passè, but are as much in effect today as on the day He first set them before man. Jesus said, "I tell you the truth, until heaven and earth disappear, not the smallest letter, not the least stroke of a pen, will by any means disappear from the Law until everything is accomplished" (Matt. 5:18). We are not to depend on our feelings when deciding right and wrong, but on God's revealed truth, for "there is a way that seems right to a man, but in the end it leads to death" (Prov. 14:12).

The Bible also declares that, contrary to what may appear to be the case, God is in control of His universe. He has a plan for it and no one can frustrate His purpose.

> The Lord Almighty has sworn, "Surely, as I have planned, so it will be, and as I have purposed, so it will stand. . . . This is the plan determined for the whole world; this is the hand stretched out over all nations. For the Lord Almighty has purposed, and who can thwart him? His hand is stretched out, and who can turn it back?" (Isa. 14:24, 26–27)

As for our unlimited personal freedom, that is nonsense. The first recorded words God spoke to Adam were on this very subject:

> And the LORD God commanded the man, "You are free to eat from any tree in the garden; but you must not eat from the tree of the knowledge of good and evil, for when you eat of it you will surely die" (Gen. 2:16–17).

Adam's freedom was not curtailed because of the demands of society—not even Eve yet shared the garden with him (Gen. 2:22). Man's freedom is limited because that is the way God wants it; it is apparently better for us that way. With God, everything is *not* permitted.

Many Paths Away From God

If we are learning anything in Ecclesiastes, it is that although there may be only one Way to God (John 14:6), there are countless paths away from Him. Jesus said, "Wide is the gate and broad is the road that leads to destruction, and many enter through it. But small is the gate and narrow the road that leads to life, and only a few find it" (Matt. 7:13–14).

We tend to look on those who hold existentialist views as a threat to our way of life, and they are. But they are also people in pain. Their world is one of disorder and tragedy. They often identify with downtrodden elements of society, as Solomon expresses in Ecclesiastes 4:1:

> Again I looked and saw all the oppression that was taking place under the sun: I saw the tears of the oppressed—and they have no comforter; power was on the side of their oppressors—and they have no comforter.

This sympathy can sometimes make us uncomfortable if we are guilty of a lack of concern for the outcasts of society. Existentialists also tend to side with lawbreakers out of concern for their restricted freedom, and this angers us. Their "passionate choices" can just as easily lead them into terrorism as into drugs or charity work, and this frightens us.

A Christian's Response

Yet through it all they are lost souls, made in the image of God but estranged from Him, sheep without a shepherd. They have made themselves enemies of God and have proclaimed Him dead, but the living God has made His enemies into His friends before, and He can do so again (Rom. 5:10). We can pity people who are so far from the joyful life God intends for us, but our *feelings* will do no more for them than their feelings are doing. Only the Holy Spirit, using the truth of God that we may be able to bring to such people, can do the work of convicting them of sin and convincing them of the truth (John 16:7–11).

Our job is to become so thoroughly saturated with God's truth through the study of His Word that we can recognize erroneous thinking when we encounter it and can become intelligent ambassadors for Him in the existentialist's strange world. Jesus prayed for this very power for us in John 17:

> My prayer is not that you take them out of the world but that you protect them from the evil one. They are not of the world, even as I am not of it. Sanctify them by the truth; your word is truth. As you sent me into the world, I have sent them into the world (vv. 15–18).

We are not to be fearful in the face of confusing modern philosophies but to trust in Jesus' words, "But take heart! I have overcome the world" (John 16:33).

* * * *

FINDING THE MEANING

1. Look up *existentialism* and *nihilism* in a dictionary. What do they mean? _____

   _____

   _____

   _____

2. What kinds of art seem to you to express existentialist philosophies? _____

   _____

3. For what purpose and future is creation heading? (See Romans 8:19–23.) _____

   _____

4. Where did man's dissatisfaction with the world, his feelings of frustration, pain, and struggle begin? From what do they result? (See Genesis 3:17–19.) _____

   _____

   _____

5. How would you answer a person who said, "God cannot be a loving God if He causes all this pain and suffering to go on in His world." _____

   _____

   _____

6. In what areas of life do you find people making decisions on the basis of feelings rather than on principles gleaned from the study of Scripture? _____

   _____

   _____

7. In what areas of life do you find God's absolute standards of right and wrong being watered down? _____

   _____

   _____

8. How would you answer a person who justifies license by saying, "It's a free country"? _____

   _____

   _____

9. What is the trouble with existentialism? _____

   _____

   _____

7

THE TROUBLE WITH STATUS

Ecclesiastes 4:4–16; 5:8–9; 6:1–2, 7:21–22

If existentialism is a difficult philosophy for Christians to grasp, Solomon's next topic is one they understand all too well, for the drive for status is probably the primary motivating factor in our culture. Most free societies, where the Christian gospel can be preached without fear of reprisal, are also competitive societies, ones that put a great emphasis on the achievement of the individual. To some extent this is a result of the Christian ethic. The Bible commands us to use our God-given abilities wisely, to earn our own bread, and often implies that God rewards with abundance those who are faithful to Him.

But most of us find it difficult to keep our attention fixed solely on fulfilling *God's* will for our lives. Instead our eyes stray to our neighbors in order to assess how well we are doing in comparison to them. Our motives in our labors become tainted with the desire not only to have as much as others have, but to have more. We not only want *God's* approval for our achievements (Matt. 25:21), we also want wide recognition from *others* as well. We become interested not only in accomplishments but also in appearances (Matt. 6:1–6).

Solomon put his finger on the real issue when he stated, "And I saw that all labor and all achievement spring from man's envy of his neighbor. This too is meaningless, a chasing after the wind" (4:4). If we are continually trying to get more and achieve more we can be guilty of greed. When we begin comparing ourselves with others and attempting to stay ahead of them in position or possessions, we are in a contest for status.

Some cultures grant status to those of exalted birth, or advanced age, or superior learning, and to some extent we do also. But we reserve the highest standing for those who wield the most power in government and industry, and who have amassed the greatest amount of wealth.

Before the advent of television, information about how the rich and powerful lived and about all the products available was spotty and regional. Styles in one part of the nation were not necessarily followed in another. Certainly the drive for status was evident, but it was more confined to the local scene. Now television has broadened our horizons and informed us of all there is to desire everywhere. Our lifestyle is in competition not only with that of our neighbors but with strangers thousands of miles away. It is not only the members of the jet set who must wear designer clothes in order to be accepted by each other; our eight-year-olds in our local schools now feel pressure to wear the right labels on their jeans and shoes. Children, bombarded with advertising in their homes from infancy, are learning the power of status symbols early these days, and their whole approach to life is affected, as is that of their parents.

Some Class Structure Inevitable

There is no way of avoiding the formation of many of the natural levels of society that arise from position or achievement. Kings, elected officials, judges always have more influence. People of great intelligence and learning are more respected and often more persuasive. The rich have advantages of power, possessions, and health over the poor. These predictable distinctions, however, are not the primary stumbling block for Christians as long as we are free to pursue our own goals, for few of us expect or even desire to become especially wealthy or famous. Our battles against envy are fought on a much less impressive field—over office locations and job titles at work, and over square footage and gadgets at home.

However, if we begin to feel thwarted in life we can become bitter about the fact that some people simply have more ability, better opportunities, or a more helpful temperament than we have. Without faith in God, the natural divisions and seeming inequities of life can make us feel that we had better work even harder, become more ruthless and single-minded, do whatever must be done to gain more status for ourselves. But the Christian hears different advice from the Word of God about how to respond to the pressures of society:

> But seek first his kingdom and his righteousness, and all these things will be given to you as well (Matt. 6:33).
> I have learned the secret of being content in any and every situation, whether well fed or hungry, whether living in plenty or in want. I can do everything through him who gives me strength (Phil. 4:12–13).

The Christian also can receive some timely warnings from a man who lived at the top, King Solomon, warnings that should cause us to wonder if exalted status is worth the price it exacts.

Success Is a Hard Taskmaster

Staying ahead of others demands a great expenditure of energy; maintaining a position at the front of the pack is a grueling business. We can get into a work syndrome where we desire more and more responsibility but forget why we are working, making the job an end in itself (4:6–8). Men can begin with a goal of providing well for their families, but end up pushing family life aside in order to gain promotions and the approval of bosses at work. Even the person with no family to support has found himself with "no end to his toil, yet his eyes were not content with his wealth. 'For whom am I toiling,' he asked, 'and why am I depriving myself of enjoyment?'" (v. 8).

The competitive atmosphere of the business world can be so hectic as to allow us little time for pleasure, for reassessment of goals, or for gaining a clear insight into what effects such an environment may be having on our personalities. Women who desire to go back to work in order "to be where the action is" may not recognize the subtle but perceptible hardening of their spirits, attitudes, and speech that can result from the daily influence found even in traditionally female occupations. No one guards their tongues because of the presence of women any more. In fact, from my own observations and the witness of acquaintances, it seems that today females have taken the lead in initiating vile conversation around the coffee pots and lunch tables of our businesses. The status gained by acquiring a responsible position or by being able to afford more possessions can cost us dearly in other areas of our lives. "Better one handful with tranquillity than two handfuls with toil and chasing after wind" (v. 6).

If God wants us to be in a certain position, He will get us there without our selling our souls, cheating our families or others, or compromising our Christian principles or witness. If we find that in seeking status we are neglecting worship, or

Bible study, or tithing, or being available to people in need, if our desire for success is really our lord, we should confess with the psalmist:

> Man is a mere phantom as he goes to and fro;
>   He bustles about, but only in vain;
>   he heaps up wealth, not knowing who will get it.
> "But now, Lord, what do I look for?
>   My hope is in you.
> Save me from all my transgressions;
>   do not make me the scorn of fools" (39:6–8).

It's Lonely at the Top

We tend to feel unsympathetic when show business personalities complain about the problems of being a star. We doubt if we would mind having crowds flocking for our autographs, having the finest accommodations everywhere, eating and dressing in nothing but the best, and making millions. But Solomon reminds us that status often sets a person apart from others and makes his position a lonely one. Whom can a king, a star, or a corporation president trust? How can they know who wants to be near them merely for personal gain or who has their best interests at heart? If limited success can alienate long-time friends because of envy on the part of one, or pride and conceit on the part of the other, what would national acclaim do?

People at the top often think, and correctly so, that others are hoping to replace them the moment they slip. "If one falls down, his friend can help him up. But pity the man who falls and has no one to help him up!" (4:10). The families of famous and powerful people experience even more stress and fragmentation than the average household. Superficial family relationships seem to be the order of the day, and of course these never satisfy the deep human need for real love. "Also, if two lie down together, they will keep warm. But how can one keep warm alone? Though one may be overpowered, two can defend themselves. A cord of three strands is not quickly broken" (vv. 11–12).

Ordinary people also find that they can have more wealth, possessions, and honor than others but not be able to enjoy them (6:1–2). This is because at its deepest level the human heart was not designed to be satisfied by the trappings of society, but by those things that money and status can never provide. "A man's life does not consist in the abundance of his possessions" (Luke 12:15). We can eat the world's food and not be satisfied (Micah 6:14), and drink at the world's well and be thirsty again (John 4:13–14). However, if we seek the kingdom of God first, He promises that our satisfaction will be deep and lasting whether He chooses to add honor and status to our lives or not (Matt. 5:6; 6:31–33).

Leaders Are Always Criticized

As Solomon surely knew from his own experience, those who enjoy superior status also receive much criticism. In Ecclesiastes 4:13–16, he shows that an old king who does not listen to warnings can be called foolish, and that even his successor will not hold the people's favor permanently. If the new young king has arisen from poverty and hardship, he may at first be hailed as a true representative of the people. But in 10:16–17, Solomon shows that such a person can be unprepared for leadership and thus open to criticism, while a king of noble birth would have the background to rule wisely. Obviously, people will always find something to gripe about.

Those who aspire to leadership positions must expect to be judged, just as they themselves have judged others. "Do not pay attention to every word people say," Solomon cautions, "or you may hear your servant cursing you—for you know in your heart that many times you yourself have cursed others" (7:21–22). James echoes, "Not many of you should presume to be teachers, my brothers, because you know that we who teach will be judged more strictly" (3:1). Yet people do desire positions of status even when their personalities are not ones that can withstand the pressure of disapproval.

Virtually every decision a leader makes displeases someone. Everyone in a position of authority makes mistakes, has personality problems and character flaws. When we hold an office where we are closely scrutinized by others, imperfections surface and are magnified by those who are opposed, or jealous, or hoping to take our place.

Always Another Rung to the Ladder

If we learn anything in life, it is that there is always someone who can do anything better than we can. You may sing beautifully, but there is someone whose voice is even more versatile. You may sew clothes flawlessly, but someone else can also tailor her husband's suits. You may get more votes this time, but lose the next election. No sports record stands forever.

Even in victory, we never have so much status that we are secure against someone with more power. Public business can be delayed, Solomon says, because "one official is eyed by a higher one, and over them both are others higher still" (5:8). The king or queen has to answer to Parliament, a president to Congress or the Supreme Court, a corporation head to stockholders, or a board of directors, or consumers. The show business personality is at the mercy of producers, investors, box-office receipts, and record purchasers.

No one ever reaches the top rung of the ladder. If keeping up appearances is crucial to us, we can never relax, for new status symbols come onto the market every day. Expensive and unique cars, boats, airplanes, summer homes, horses, newer fashions, beautiful jewelry, vacation cruises; the list is endless. Not only does someone always rank higher, but someone always has finer possessions as well. The person who needs high status in order to thrive is in a precarious position, one that depends upon the opinions of those above him and the possession of ever-changing symbols of social prominence.

Jesus and Status

Jesus had the ultimate opportunity for status—that of being the ruler of all kingdoms of the earth rather than the crucified Savior of the world. In Matthew 4:8–10 Satan showed our Lord the splendor of all the world's kingdoms and promised Him He could have them if He would only serve him. Somehow it strikes us as being easier for Jesus to reject all that than for us to relinquish our private little dreams of personal glory, whatever they may be. But Jesus' answer should be our answer whenever we feel our desires pulling us away from the center of God's will: "Away from me, Satan! For it is written: 'Worship the Lord your God, and serve him only.'"

While Jesus' temptation was on a scale beyond our comprehension, He showed that He nevertheless understands our daily struggles. He speaks in Luke 14:7–11 of such a mundane thing as being invited to dinner, and cautions us against taking a place of honor, "for a person more distinguished than you may have been invited. If so, the host . . . will come to say to you, 'Give this man your seat.'" To spare ourselves humiliation, we should rather "take the lowest place, so that when your host comes, he will say to you, 'Friend, move up to a better place.'" Jesus concludes by warning, "For everyone who exalts himself will be humbled, and he who humbles himself will be exalted."

James 2:1–4 teaches us that we are not to follow the world's standards by showing favoritism based on a person's appearance. "If you show special attention to the man wearing fine clothes . . . but say to the poor man, 'You stand there,' or, 'Sit on the floor by my feet,' have you not discriminated among yourselves and become judges of evil thoughts?" Jesus said that the trappings of wealth mean nothing to God, but that they are often a stumbling block on a person's spiritual path (Matt. 19:24). We are the ones who look on outward appearances—the Lord looks on the heart (1 Sam. 16:7).

Our labor and achievement are not to "spring from man's envy of his neighbor" but from our answer to God's call. We are supposed to be concentrating on God's will for us rather than comparing our lot with that of others. This has never been easy, even for those who have been the closest to the Lord. For when the resurrected Jesus was talking to Peter, giving him the awesome task of feeding His sheep, Peter could not resist looking at another disciple and asking, "Lord, what about him?" Jesus answered, "What is that to you? You must follow me" (John 21:21–22). When we start comparing the life God has given us with that of someone else and begin to long for more success, honor, and status, we should think of all the pitfalls involved and recall the Lord's words of calm correction and command, "What is that to you? Follow me!"

* * * *

FINDING THE MEANING

1. How is status related to 1 John 2:16? _____

_____

_____

2. How can even religious people express their desire for status? (Read Matthew 23:5–7.) _____

_____

_____

3. How are Christians supposed to handle the issue of status in the church? (See Matthew 20:25–28.) _____

_____

4. If we are not to yearn for status ourselves, are we to grant it to others? (See Romans 12:10; 13:7.) _____

_____

5. Who, specifically, are Christians supposed to honor? How are they to show that honor? (See Exodus 20:12; Romans 13:6–7; Philippians 2:29–30; 1 Timothy 5:17–21.) _____

_____

_____

_____

_____

6. Do you hesitate to show honor to those to whom it is due? What do you need to change, what actions do you need to take? _____

_____

_____

7. Is your church obedient to the commands in 1 Timothy 5:17–21? What actions does your church need to take?

_____

_____

8. In what areas of your personal life do you struggle most with the desire for status? _____

_____

_____

9. What are God's rules for gaining honor? (See Proverbs 15:33; 18:12; 21:21; 22:4.) _____

_____

_____

_____

_____

10. What does a person give up in achieving high social status? _____

_____

11. What is the trouble with status? _____

_____

_____

8

THE TROUBLE WITH GOOD INTENTIONS

Ecclesiastes 5:1–7

There are thousands of people sitting in our churches every Sunday who are there for the wrong reasons; but they mean well. They attend worship because they believe it is the right thing to do, because they want to be counted as a moral person, because they want to fulfill an obligation they think they owe their Maker. They may also come to see friends and be seen, to enhance a business or social image, or to satisfy an aesthetic need by listening to beautiful music in a lovely setting. None of these are sinister motives. Such attitudes are the result of the natural reasoning of people who think they know what God requires without having personally studied the matter.

King Saul meant well, too, when he brought "the best of the sheep and cattle, the fat calves and lambs—everything that was good" back with him from war, some of which he intended to use for sacrifices (1 Sam. 15:9). Saul was very pleased with himself as he greeted Samuel the priest and said cheerily, "The LORD bless you! I have carried out the LORD's instructions" (v. 13). Just as with many people today, Saul thought that God doesn't really care whether you obey Him fully. Saul was wrong.

What God had told Saul was, "Go, attack the Amalekites and totally destroy everything that belongs to them. Do not spare them; put to death men and women, children and infants, cattle and sheep, camels and donkeys" (v. 3). When Samuel accused Saul of disobeying these commands, Saul replied, "But I did obey the LORD. I went on the mission the LORD assigned me. I completely destroyed the Amalekites and brought back Agag their king. The soldiers took sheep and cattle from the plunder, the best of what was devoted to God, in order to sacrifice them to the LORD your God at Gilgal" (vv. 20–21).

Ignorance No Excuse

Obviously, Saul had either been a poor listener or a purposeful sinner; he had either neglected to pay attention to the Word of God or he had directly disobeyed. Either way he was at fault.

Ecclesiastes 5:1 warns, "Guard your steps when you go to the house of God. Go near to listen rather than to offer the sacrifice of fools, who do not know that they do wrong." Notice that even though people may not *know* they are doing wrong, they are not excused; "they do wrong." They may mean well, but their good intentions will not save them or please God. They may be completely satisfied in their own minds (saying in effect, "But I did obey the Lord!"), and feel as cheerful as Saul did about their standing with God, but if they are not obeying God's commands they are fooling themselves.

Saul tried to offer "the sacrifice of fools"; he tried to make his own rules and worship God on his own terms, even though it should have been obvious that God would never accept the sacrifice of animals brought back in disobedience to His commands! Yet many people think the same way today. They feel that God is happy to have whatever attention they are willing to give Him, whether they are obeying Him or not. The fact is that God utterly rejects such pseudo-worship. As Samuel said to Saul, "Because you have rejected the word of the LORD, he has rejected you as king" (1 Sam. 15:23). Since the Lord takes the matter of worship so seriously, how can we "guard our steps" so that we can approach the house of God in a way pleasing to Him?

We Must Identify Our Motives

Most of us never stop to think through our reasons for going to church. What is our motivation? What do we hope to find there? We often cannot say. Neither do we have any clear idea about what the God we are supposedly worshiping is like. Most people have a pathetic sort of God in mind: ineffectual, dependent upon humans for action, easily pleased by little bits of attention. They come by their ideas about God from such things as conversations in the homes in which they were raised, scraps of sermons heard while turning radio and TV dials, caricatures of religious doings portrayed in movies, pronouncements of various church leaders, and the remarks of schoolteachers and friends.

The result is that our religious ideas are often a hodgepodge of the various opinions to which we have been exposed, usually those that sound the most broadminded and moderate. Any statement that involves the name of God and demands little from people tends to gain wide acceptance. Solomon comes up with a statement sure to please:

> Do not be overrighteous, neither be overwise—why destroy yourself? Do not be overwicked, and do not be a fool—why

die before your time? It is good to grasp the one and not let go of the other. The man who fears God will avoid all extremes (7:16–18).

The Bible says that we should set aside our uninformed opinions and "draw near to listen" when we go to church so that our foolishness will be corrected and our ignorance overcome.

We Must Listen Carefully

As we have seen in our study of Ecclesiastes, humans have had some strange ideas about what constitutes right living; and Solomon has pointed out the fallacy of each one. If we would "guard our steps," we must be wary of any religious statements that do not match up with the clear teachings of the whole of God's Word. The Bible contains approximately thirteen hundred pages of information that God wants those who worship Him to understand. The Bible was not written so that a few scholars could mine its depths in musty cells, but so that you and I could know how to be friends with God. As Saul found out, you have to pay *close attention* if you want to know what God requires, and you have to *obey* Him if you want His approval.

Jesus, who is God (John 1:1, 14), said that only those who both hear His words and put them into practice could be compared to the wise man who builds his house upon a rock. Those who hear His words but do not act upon them are foolish. But we cannot obey someone until we know what he has commanded—and here is where the trouble lies. Too many people are content to believe what the man preaching in church or on television *says* God said. They don't find out what God said for themselves. They prefer to have an inspirational talk, an intellectual discussion, or an emotional experience rather than expend the effort to prove or disprove the truth of what they hear.

We guard our steps when we listen carefully and then check up on the people who teach us and make sure that they are not twisting the Scriptures (2 Peter 3:16–17). The Bible says the people of a town called Berea were "of more noble character" than citizens of other towns because they not only "received the message with great eagerness," but also "examined the Scriptures every day to see if what Paul said was true" (Acts 17:11). The Bereans did not want to jump on the latest bandwagon, they did not want to be swayed by Paul's reputation or oratorical prowess, or by the emotion of the moment. They put in the hard work of reading the Scriptures for themselves.

It is not enough to mean well or to say, "My heart is in the right place." Our hearts can never be in the right place until we have a heart that hungers and thirsts after righteousness, a heart that desires above all else to know our Lord (Phil. 3:8–10). We will never acquire correct knowledge about God apart from the Bible. Scripture is the lamp to our feet and light to our path (Ps. 119:105) that guards our steps as we hold everything we hear up to its light.

We Must Be Slow to Speak

Women are in general more verbal than men. We share problems with each other more readily, seek help and advice more quickly from professionals and nonprofessionals alike (though we spend more time telling than listening), and can express ourselves more easily than men can. Often we think that not even God can understand what we are thinking and feeling until we have explained our concern to Him six different ways. Especially women, then, should take seriously the admonitions of Ecclesiastes 5:2–3 and guard their mouths as well as their steps before God.

I have been in groups where women took over the discussion and the leaders were forced to take very firm measures to bring the group back to the intended topic. Yet women tend to become indignant when Paul, writing "the Lord's command," tells women to wait until they get home and to ask their own husbands if they have questions but to keep quiet in church (1 Cor. 14:33–37). God wants us to stop trying to express ourselves and to listen. We cannot hear and speak at the same time.

The Bible says that women should seek "the unfading beauty of a gentle and quiet spirit, which is of great worth in God's sight" (1 Peter 3:4). Some of us talk incessantly because we are nervous or insecure. We hear ourselves prattling on about inconsequential matters and don't know how we acquired the habit. The Lord wants us to close our mouths and keep them under control so that we may not have "the speech of a fool when there are many words" (5:3).

God also desires that we be "quick to listen, slow to speak" (James 1:19) so that we will not express opinions contrary to the Word of God and harmful to others. Saul was sure he knew what God wanted in his situation, but he was wrong and so caused his men to disobey God as well. Women must be sure the advice they give to others is based on the Word of God, on what they have heard while listening to Him, and not on human insight. God hears the conversations we have in our kitchens or at work as well as those at church. He cautions us, "Do not be quick with your mouth, do not be hasty in your heart to utter anything before God" (5:2).

We Must Fulfill Our Vows

One specific type of utterance God warns us to treat most seriously is our vows. Vows are not much in fashion these days. The Old Testament gives guidelines for making and being released from vows in several places (see Num. 6; 30:1–7), but modern people tend to consider taking vows an out-moded idea.

On the contrary, vows are an integral part of our daily lives and we depend on them in a variety of ways. Witnesses in court and those making notarized statements swear to tell the truth. People in sensitive occupations are required to take a loyalty oath. Our public officials take an oath of office. Everyone who marries makes wedding vows.

The reason the subject of vows seems out of date is that people are not deadly serious anymore when they make a promise. They have good intentions, but when difficulties arise they simply break their vow. A person's word used to be a sacred trust. Failure to honor a verbal commitment resulted in being an outcast from polite society; people no longer associated with a person who had not fulfilled a debt of honor.

Today, however, vows are not worth the paper they are written on. Every air traffic controller in the United States signs an oath that he or she will not strike. Yet in August of 1981, 97 percent of them did strike, despite President Reagan's warning that they would lose their jobs and be prosecuted if they did so. The President said, "If we ever decide the oath of office isn't important to keep, how long do we have this society?"[1]

Wedding vows, taken "before God and these witnesses," "till death do us part," also seem rarely to be considered binding. A divorced columnist, writing about the deterioration of a relationship—her lifelong friendship with a housewife—seems to catch more accurately the modern view of marriage vows:

> "I guess I'm just one of those old-fashioned people who does what she promised to do on her wedding day," my friend said with a smug, self-righteous smile. She is a woman who has never realized that at 29 she couldn't keep promises made at 19. . . .
>
> To get even, I called and told her about a good Catholic

husband who'd left his wife (mother of five) for a young feminist. Secretly I think it will happen to her someday, and it will serve her right for being so damned smug about her wedding vows.[2]

God's solemn view of vows, however, is described vividly in Ecclesiastes 5:4–6. God says not to try to get out of our vows by saying, "My vow was a mistake" (v. 6). His reaction to that is to be "angry at what you say and destroy the work of your hands." He says it is better not to vow than to vow and not pay it, because such a person is both a sinner and a fool (vv. 4–5). These awesome warnings should be enough to make each of us who is married tremble and search our hearts as we consider whether we have fulfilled the vows we took:

> I do promise and covenant; before God and these witnesses; to be thy loving and faithful wife; in plenty and in want; in joy and in sorrow; in sickness and in health; as long as we both shall live.

Have we always been loving? Have we been faithful in thought as well as deed? Have we let some circumstance become an excuse for failing in our commitment? Honest answers to these questions should keep any of us from feeling smug about how we have followed through on our good intentions. They should also cause us to counsel carefully with our children as they begin to consider marriage so that they understand the seriousness and permanence of the promises they will be making.

Divorce, the ultimate rupture of one's marriage vows, is currently so readily accepted by society that we have lost sight of God's view almost entirely. God does not consider divorce an acceptable solution when things don't seem to be working out. In Malachi 2:13–16, God points to widespread divorce, the breaking of marriage covenants, as one of the reasons why He does not accept Judah's offerings. Our nation would do well to listen as the Lord explains how serious an offense He considers our breaking of vows to be:

> The LORD is acting as the witness between you and the wife of your youth, because you have broken faith with her, though she is your partner, the wife of your marriage covenant. Has not the LORD made them one? In flesh and spirit they are his. And why one? Because he was seeking godly offspring. So guard yourself in your spirit and do not break faith with the wife of your youth. "I hate divorce," says the LORD God of Israel. . . . So guard yourself in your spirit and do not break faith.

Good Intentions Are Meaningless

Solomon sums up the discussion of worship by saying, "Much dreaming and many words are meaningless. Therefore stand in awe of God" (5:7). Good intentions, like dreams and words, are not actions; and unless we follow through on our intentions, they are meaningless. We can delude ourselves by intending wonderful things and taking credit for good intentions as though they were actual deeds. We *mean* to pray, and so consider ourselves women of prayer. We *think* about helping the poor, and pat ourselves on the back for having such worthy thoughts. We approve of being obedient to all of God's Word, and feel like good Christians even though our lives *do not* conform to that Word. In short, good intentions keep us pleased with our noble thoughts and blind us to the fact that we are useless to God.

"Stand in awe of God," Solomon commands. Stop playing religious games. See the Lord for the almighty One He is. Guard your steps; guard your mouth; guard your spirit (Mal. 2:16). These commands describe the actions of an individual who is on duty for many hours rather than the careless attitude of someone who only means well. "Do not merely listen to the word, and so deceive yourselves. Do what it says" (James 1:22). "For the kingdom of God is not a matter of talk but of power" (1 Cor. 4:20).

* * * *

FINDING THE MEANING

1. What does the old saying, "The road to hell is paved with good intentions," mean to you? _____

_____

_____

2. In what areas of your life do you find it most difficult to live up to your good intentions? _____

_____

_____

3. What happened to Peter's good intentions? (See Mark 14:29–31, 66–72.) _____

_____

_____

4. How can you turn your good intentions into realities? (See Philippians 4:13.) _____

_____

_____

5. List the things we can learn about proper attitudes for services of worship from the following verses: Isaiah 1:12; Habakkuk 2:20; Matthew 6:7. _____

_____

_____

_____

6. What sometimes happens to people who come to church intending to worship and pray? (See Isaiah 42:20; Mark 14:32–41; Acts 20:7–9.) _____

_____

_____

_____

7. What about those "who do not know that they do wrong"? (See Leviticus 4:2, 22.) _____

_____

8. What happens when we talk too much? (See Proverbs 10:19; 1 Timothy 5:13; 2 Timothy 2:16.) _____

_____

_____

_____

9. Do vows made in an emotional moment count? (See Psalm 66:13–14.) _____

_____

10. What should we do if we have broken vows or not lived up to our intentions and commitments? (See Matthew 5:23–24; 1 John 1:9.) _____

_____

_____

11. What is the trouble with good intentions? _____

_____

9

THE TROUBLE WITH FATALISM

Ecclesiastes 9:1–12

Probably more people of the world adhere to fatalism than to any other religious tenet, for fatalism is a major belief not only of the Hindus and Moslems, but of the Buddhists as well. Both Hindus and Buddhists believe in *karma*: that is, the sum of all a person's existences is his inevitable destiny. Islam, the collective term for the religion of all Moslems, actually means "resignation," and is the second largest religion of the world, ranking a surprising third even in the United States.

Fatalism holds that the course of events is decreed by some metaphysical power, independent of the will or actions of individuals. Thus Solomon sets forward a fatalistic view when he states:

> All share a common destiny—the righteous and the wicked, the good and the bad, the clean and the unclean, those who offer sacrifices and those who do not. As it is with the good man, so with the sinner; as it is with those who take oaths, so with those who are afraid to take them. This is the evil in

everything that happens under the sun: The same destiny overtakes all (vv. 2–3).

Since our beliefs affect our actions, it is important to examine what effect this kind of thinking has on the everyday life of a culture. And since in recent years Western cultures have sustained an influx of Eastern religious thought in the form of gurus, transcendental meditation, yoga, and so on, it would be wise to find out in what directions such influences are taking us.

It does not require great powers of discernment to see that Eastern religions have seldom created the kind of life sought after by Christians. Millions of people in India, for example, have over the centuries been left to eke out a meager subsistence, to survive or die, with little help from their own countrymen. Rather, it has been Christian missionaries, with their emphasis on helping the needy, who have brought hospitals, schools, and basic health and farming practices to areas that had remained underdeveloped under their native religions. This is not speculation or bragging, but simple fact. Obviously, biblical beliefs have a different impact on nations than do nonbiblical ones.

Results of Resignation

Whenever a person, for whatever reason, sits back and decides to let events take their course, he or she becomes a drag on society. When a whole culture adopts the view that "whatever will be will be," the standard of living declines. The Thessalonians thought Jesus was going to return soon or perhaps had already done so (2 Thess. 2:1–2), so some decided to stop working and wait to be raptured. Paul commands them, in the name of the Lord Jesus Christ, to separate themselves from idle ones and set down the rule, "If a man will not work, he shall not eat" (3:10). He reminded them of the example of hard toil and labor he had set for them when he was with them and said that those who did not carry their share of the load were a burden on others (3:6–9).

If we decide that nothing we do can affect the direction of our lives, initiative dies and is replaced by lethargy. We will shrug off responsibility for our actions and blame fate for any negative consequences. However, the Bible clearly teaches that "each of us will give an account of himself to God" (Rom. 14:12). And when God inquires into our reason for failing to follow His revealed will, He will not be much impressed by the excuse, "It was my karma."

Two Destinies

The fatalist's argument that "all share a common destiny —the righteous and the wicked, the good and the bad, the clean and the unclean" is not a biblical concept. On the contrary, Jesus made it absolutely clear in His teachings on the wheat and tares (Matt. 13:24–30), the good and bad fish (Matt. 13:47–52), the sheep and the goats (Matt. 25:31–43), and in many other places, that the exact opposite is true. Jesus said that at the end of the age "the Son of Man will send out his angels, and they will weed out of his kingdom everything that causes sin and all who do evil. They will throw them into the fiery furnace, where there will be weeping and gnashing of teeth. Then the righteous will shine like the sun in the kingdom of their Father" (Matt. 13:42–43).

Certainly all humans die eventually, but there are two eternal destinies. Those who believe in Jesus Christ are promised eternal life (John 3:16), those who reject Him are punished not just with destruction, but with *eternal* destruction (2 Thess. 1:9), and are shut out from the presence of the Lord. The world may prefer to ignore such ominous teaching and claim that "in the grave, where you are going, there is neither working nor planning nor knowledge nor wisdom" (Eccl.

9:10), but the Word of God clearly teaches that our spirits live on and will know what is happening to us after our death.

God's Purpose Vs. Fatalism

Christians may become confused and unknowingly adopt the attitudes engendered by fatalism because they do not understand the difference between fate and the plan of God. The Bible makes it clear that God's purposes in the world will come to pass despite any human plan to the contrary:

> Many are the plans in a man's heart, but it is the LORD's purpose that prevails (Prov. 19:21).
> The LORD foils the plans of the nations; he thwarts the purposes of the people. But the plans of the LORD stand firm forever, the purposes of his heart through all generations (Ps. 33:10–11).

The difference between fatalism and Christianity lies in the fact that God only plans things for the ultimate *good* of His children, and that He has *revealed* His purposes in the Bible. Thus as Christians we do not need to float along aimlessly on the one hand or attempt to nullify God's plan on the other. Instead we can join with Him—become, in fact, fellow workers (1 Cor. 3:9)—and make our lives count for something as we fall in with His will. The fatalist says, "As fish are caught in a cruel net, or birds are taken in a snare, so men are trapped by evil times that fall unexpectedly upon them" (Eccl. 9:12). But the Christian meets the hardships of life with the exhortation of James: "Consider it pure joy, my brothers, whenever you face trials of many kinds, because you know that the testing of your faith develops perseverance. Perseverance must finish its work so that you may be mature and complete, not lacking anything" (1:2–4). We know we are not victims of chance, but recipients of the love of the God who makes all things work together for our good (Rom. 8:28).

While uncertainty about the outcome may cause a fatalist

to quit trying, the Christian has the following instructions: "Sow your seed in the morning, and at evening let not your hands be idle, for you do not know which will succeed, whether this or that, or whether both will do equally well" (Eccl. 11:6). For if the believer does not know which of his works will flourish, he trusts that God does. We may plant and water, but it is God who gives the increase (1 Cor. 3:6–7). The Christian is content to rest, not in the mindless twists of fate, but in the greater wisdom of the Creator God: "As you do not know the path of the wind, or how the body is formed in a mother's womb, so you cannot understand the work of God, the Maker of all things" (Eccl. 11:5).

The fatalist sees life as the attempt of a blind person to grope along through an endless night, powerless to avoid pitfalls and at the mercy of chance encounters. But Christians know that God has revealed the path we should walk and has given us the light of His Word to illumine our way. In Christ He has cured our blindness and given us eyes to see clearly. He has planted within us the Holy Spirit to continually unfold His plan to us (1 Cor. 2:9–11). The fact that God's purposes will come to pass does not make the Christian feel ineffectual and passive, but confident and energetic.

Believers agree with all in Ecclesiastes 9:11 except the last line. We know that "the race is not to the swift or the battle to the strong," for the Lord has told us that He purposely "chose the weak things of the world to shame the strong" (1 Cor. 1:27). We know that food does not necessarily come to the wise, nor wealth to the brilliant, nor favor to the learned. But it is not time and *chance* that overtake all men, but time and the loving plan of God.

Results of Fatalism

The fatalists' view inevitably fosters lives of inconsistent morality and despair: immorality because there is no reason to be good, especially when it is inconvenient, if both the good and bad have the same fate; despair, because living seems so pointless and death so imminent and menacing. Attempts at hopeful living such as in Ecclesiastes 9:4 sound pathetic: "Even a live dog is better off than a dead lion"! Preoccupation with the fleeting pleasures of food, drink, and clothing seem to be all that assuages their suffering spirits (9:7–9), for the ever-present specter of death haunts their thoughts (9:3, 4, 5, 6, 10, 12). Life for the fatalist is more something to be endured as painlessly as possible than truly enjoyed: "Enjoy life with your wife, whom you love, all the days of this meaningless life that God has given you under the sun—all your meaningless days. For this is your lot in life and in your toilsome labor under the sun" (9:9).

In contrast, Jesus promises a superior quality of life *now* to those who come to Him (John 10:10), as well as fullness of joy (John 15:11), a living hope (1 Peter 1:3), and true satisfaction in doing good (Matt. 5:6).

In English, the words *fate* and *father* are very much alike. But to be resigned to one's fate is a world away from giving oneself into the care of a loving Father. From *fate,* we get the words *fateful* (portentous, ominous, ruinous) and *fatal* (deadly, mortal, disastrous). *Father,* however, fills our minds with images of someone who shows personal interest, who takes responsibility for the welfare of his children, who protects, corrects, and loves them.

The fatalist's view of our ultimate destiny is indeed an ominous one: "Man's fate is like that of the animals; the same fate awaits them both: As one dies, so does the other. All have the same breath; man has no advantage over the animal. Everything is meaningless" (Eccl. 3:19–20).

Christians anticipate something quite different, for Jesus said that our heavenly Father has provided for our eternal destiny in a manner befitting a treasured member of His family. "In my Father's house are many rooms. . . . I am going there to prepare a place for you" (John 14:2). We know that this kind of loving care for us does not begin when we die, but is ours from the moment we become His child. "Surely goodness and love will follow me all the days of my life, and I will dwell in the house of the LORD forever" (Ps. 23:6).

* * * *

FINDING THE MEANING

1. Look up *fatalism* in a dictionary. What does it mean?

   _____

2. What influences of Eastern religions do you see in our nation's life today? What impact might immigrants who hold these beliefs have upon our country? _____

   _____

   _____

3. What do you know about the growth of the Muslims, Hare Krishna, yoga, and transcendental meditation in our country? What news articles dealing with these subjects can you find? _____

   _____

   _____

4. What would the Word of God say about clearing our minds of all thought by constantly repeating a word or "mantra"? (See Matthew 6:7; Philippians 4:6–8.)

   _____

   _____

   _____

5. List ways in which God's unchangeable plan for His children differs from fate. (See Ephesians 1:3–14.)

   _____

   _____

6. According to the testimony of one who resisted God's plan for a while, what does such disobedience feel like? (See Acts 26:12–14.) _____

   _____

7. How did God arrange for Saul to conform to His plan for Saul's life? (See Acts 9:1–19.) _____

   _____

   _____

8. What was Paul's attitude concerning God's plan for his life? (See Philippians 3:3–11.) _____

   _____

9. Are you fighting God's will in some area of your life? If so, what would Paul's experiences lead you to expect in your own life? _____

   _____

   _____

10. Review all portions of Ecclesiastes cited in this chapter. How can we decide whether they come from "under the sun" or "above the sun"? _____

11. What is the trouble with fatalism? _____

   _____

   _____

10

THE TROUBLE WITH YOUTH

Ecclesiastes 11:7–12:2

Solomon once again proves that ancient and modern thinking do not differ greatly from one another when he compares youth and age to light and darkness (11:7–8; 12:1–2). Youth, like light, is sweet and pleasing, we insist, while age denotes "days of darkness" or "days of trouble," years when we can only say, "I find no pleasure in them." Since youth constitutes only about one-third of our life, such a definition would mean that the greater part of our days on earth fall into the category of darkness.

This view of life is especially prevalent among young people themselves. From their perspective, real living ceases shortly after reaching eighteen. They have great difficulty envisioning adults as people with exciting dreams, romantic passions, or interesting opportunities, and usually reject any attempts to stir their imaginations along these lines.

In Ecclesiastes 11:8 Solomon challenges the idea that people's early years are the only good ones they will ever know. Such a gloomy view fosters a lack of restraint on the part of the young, and increases their tendency to feel a frantic need to experience everything life has to offer before age and oblivion overtake them.

Solomon cautions young people against reckless living by reminding them that they are accountable for the actions of their youth as well as for those of later years (11:9). He knows that there are many years of regret ahead for those who succumb to the temptations of the world during their teen-age years.

Young People in the Bible

A surprising number of the important characters in Scripture were young people, and the Bible records their problems, weaknesses, and failures as well as their successes. Joseph's lack of humility about his dreams and smugness over his favored status with his father goaded his brothers into selling him into slavery. Samuel was separated from his parents at a very young age but accepted his life with an old priest at the temple. David, although anointed while a teen-ager to be the next king, refused to take matters into his own hands, but spent years in hardship waiting for God to advance him at His own time. Jeremiah was "only a child" (Jer. 1:6–7) when God called him to carry His word to the nations. Esther was a young orphan, raised by an uncle, who went from obscurity to the office of queen with such modesty and grace that she was able to gain the favor necessary to rescue the entire Jewish population. Mary was a young maiden when she set aside her plans for a normal life with her betrothed and declared to the angel Gabriel, "I am the Lord's servant. May it be to me as you have said" (Luke 1:38). John Mark could not endure the hardships of missionary life, leaving Paul and Barnabas and returning to his hometown (Acts 15:37–39). Timothy was a timid young man who needed Paul's continuing encouragement in order to overcome his fears and lead the church placed in his care (1 Tim. 4:12).

Scripture tells us that all of these young people, even those who failed initially, ended up being used in a special way by the Lord. They encountered the same array of difficult problems experienced by adolescents today, but by "remembering their Creator in the days of their youth" (Eccl. 12:1) they emerged victorious. The Creator has several things he wants the young to remember.

Remember to Learn From the Experience of Others

According to 1 Corinthians 10:11, our God had the life stories of people like those mentioned above recorded for a definite purpose: "These things happened to them as examples and were written down as warnings for us, on whom the fulfillment of the ages has come."

One of the problems young people face is that the lack of experience makes them vulnerable to life's snares. A mature Christian may be able to say, "I was young and now I am old, yet I have never seen the righteous forsaken or their children begging bread" (Ps. 37:25), but young people have little experience that helps them face the present with faith. No matter how much head knowledge a youth has, the knowledge must be tested and applied to specific life situations before he or she can claim it to be true from personal experience. But such a person can gain much strength and courage by seeing how the Lord has proved Himself in the lives of others.

In their better moments, young people realize that they can avoid much pain by listening to the wise counsel of adults who have survived the trials of life. They also see around them the sad examples of unwise living and hope to avoid that kind of future for themselves. What they find difficult is to believe that the elders' assessment of the particular situation facing them *now* is the sound one, especially if it differs from their own. For example, a young man may agree that loose women must be avoided (Prov. 7:7 ff.), and may be aware of acquaintances who have committed the sin of fornication. But convincing him that a particular female who has caught his eye falls into the "loose woman" category is another task altogether.

Having to heed parents and teachers is a constant source of irritation to those trying to grow from childhood into independence. The role of perpetual learner rankles. Yet the Bible characterizes a person's early life as a time of training in scriptural principles in preparation for adult responsibility (2 Tim. 3:15–17). The young are told to submit to the instruction of their elders in humility (1 Peter 5:5), and to ignore such counsel is to endanger their own futures.

Remember: The Creator Judges

Another overpowering reason why young people should stifle rebellion and heed their parents and teachers is that they will have to account for their actions before their Creator. Solomon says that young people should follow their dreams carefully, because "for all these things God will bring you to judgment" (11:9). Unwise living will not only wreak havoc with their present, but will also affect their earthly and heavenly future. Writing on this subject, James Dobson quotes his father:

> Desire is like a river. As long as it flows within the banks of God's will—be the current strong or weak—all is well. But when it flows over those boundaries and seeks other channels, then disaster lurks in the rampage.[1]

Remember: Youth Is a Joyful Time

The real purpose for all of God's warnings and prohibitions is to keep us from error so that we can have an enjoyable life that glorifies Him on this earth. The image of God as a supernatural spoilsport is one of Satan's greatest triumphs. Jesus said, "I have come that they may have life, and have it to the full" (John 10:10), and "they" includes young people.

A major part of the Book of Ecclesiastes is a study of what does *not* make a person happy. Solomon has already showed that possessions, pleasure, money, status—in short, all the things that constitute most youthful dreams of success—are meaningless, futile life goals. So when he says, "Follow the ways of your heart and whatever your eyes see," he cannot be issuing a license for hedonistic living, for he immediately follows this statement with his warning of judgment. Rather, he is simply stating that a joyful life is a good thing.

Perhaps adults are the ones who need the message of these verses the most, for children usually do not need to be encouraged to have fun. But parents may need to be reminded that one of our goals for our children should be joyful, happy childhood protected from the heavy burdens of life. The "days of darkness" will come soon enough, and "they will be many" (11:8).

We see at times a tendency on the part of parents to envy the carefree existence of their children and to squelch their high spirits and rosy outlook. Certainly the young need to learn to take life seriously, but the events of life prevent anyone from growing up without their share of sobering moments. Friends move away, relatives and pets die, the demands of school tax their abilities. Other children tease and fight, parents are too harsh or indifferent, illnesses afflict. Young people have plenty to worry them. Perhaps loving parents, rather than dumping their adult worries on the young, should say instead, "Be happy, young man, while you are young, and let your heart give you joy in the days of your youth" (11:9).

Remember the Days of Darkness

The young have had little enough chance to enjoy their lives throughout human history. They have suffered famine, drought, pestilence, and flood along with their elders. At this moment, children in many places around the world are experiencing every imaginable evil because they are powerless to protect themselves. Even in affluent societies, children suffer from the results of ungodly living on the part of the adults in their lives and have become the target of criminal elements. The threat of war, nuclear or otherwise, intrudes upon the plans our young people make for their futures. News media faithfully chronicle murders, fires, scandals, and uprisings here and abroad, and our so-called entertainment industry portrays every kind of tragedy in gory detail. Our young people would have to be sheltered indeed to escape learning about the misfortunes of life.

But Solomon says that such knowledge can serve a useful purpose. Remembering the days of darkness gives us a perspective from which to appreciate the joyful times. By coming to grips with the bad as well as the good, children, as well as adults, will learn to endure the night with more fortitude and be more grateful for the day.

The Disadvantages of Being Young

It is fashionable for adults to try to look as youthful as possible these days. But the young, as they have ever done, still do everything they can to look older. They know that their firm, supple bodies do not make up for the disadvantages of their lack of years. They realize all too well that they possess insufficient knowledge, experience, sense of perspective, and power to protect themselves sufficiently or to change their situation in life.

Some adults, faced with the prospect of advancing age,

may truly envy the young. But Solomon says that the exaltation of youthfulness is just another of our vain illusions. The energy and enthusiasm of youth, he says, are of no lasting benefit either, and we are foolish to wish to be other than we are.

So then, banish anxiety from your heart and cast off the troubles of your body, for youth and vigor are meaningless (11:10).

* * * *

FINDING THE MEANING

1. What is more important to success than youth? (See Joshua 1:7; Isaiah 40:30–31.) _____

_____

_____

2. How can young people avoid sinning? (See Psalm 119:9, 11; 2 Timothy 2:22.) _____

_____

_____

3. If the young are to "overcome the evil one" and "be strong," what must they do? (See 1 John 2:13–16.)

_____

_____

4. How did Daniel and three other young men go about remaining faithful to the Lord in an intimidating situation? (See Daniel 1:3–17.) _____

_____

_____

5. What is a mother's responsibility with regard to her children's preparation for godly living? (See Deuteronomy 6:6–7; 2 Timothy 1:5; 3:14.) _____

    _____

    _____

6. What would a godly mother hope each of her children would be able to say? (See Psalm 71:17.) _____

    _____

    _____

7. How can parents make childhood a troubled time for their children? _____

    _____

8. What can we do to give our children the kind of childhood God desires for them? _____

    _____

9. What could be the results in the life of a woman who is preoccupied with a desire for youthfulness? _____

    _____

    _____

10. What is the trouble with youth? _____

    _____

    _____

11

THE TROUBLE WITH AGE

Ecclesiastes 12:1–8

Of the thirty-nine books that comprise the Old Testament, only five do not pertain to the history of the Jewish people. These five books, Job, Psalms, Proverbs, Ecclesiastes, and the Song of Songs, are called the poetry section of the Bible. The majority of the Book of Ecclesiastes is written in the form of verse, and nowhere does Solomon reach greater heights of poetic imagery than when he turns to the topic of growing old.

In view of Solomon's statement, "However many years a man may live, let him enjoy them all" (11:8), his recital of the prospects of old age in chapter 12 is more than a little daunting. As his description of a person's waning years unfolds, one can readily understand why he says in verse 1, "I find no pleasure in them"!

According to this account, the body totally turns traitor to the person inhabiting it. Hands, "keepers of the house," tremble, and the body stoops (v. 3). Teeth, "the grinders, cease because they are few," and the eyes, "those looking through the windows," "grow dim" (v. 3). Ears, "the doors to the street are closed and the sound of grinding fades" (v. 4). Sleep is elusive as the elderly awaken with the birds (v. 4), and fears of various kinds increase (v. 5). Sexual desire fades and dies (v. 5). With such a future to look forward to, it is no wonder people want to deny the reality of advancing years as long as possible!

Three Possible Ends

The problem is, unless the Lord returns or we die young, we *will* grow old. If Eve (or someone else later) had not disobeyed God, all the people on this planet would be munching away on the fruit of the Tree of Life and living forever instead of slowly deteriorating as the result of sin, and dying (Gen. 3:22–24). But sin and death are now facts to be reckoned with, and we are called by God to approach every phase of our lives in an attitude of faith.

It is possible that Jesus Christ may return before we die (1 Thess. 4:16–17). Solomon's use of the phrases "before the days of trouble come," and "before the sun and the light and the moon and the stars grow dark" (vv. 1–2) remind us of various descriptions of the end times in Scripture.

> See, the day of the LORD is coming—a cruel day, with wrath and fierce anger. . . . The stars of heaven and their constellations will not show their light. The rising sun will be darkened, and the moon will not give its light (Isa. 13:9–10).

The prophets Joel (2:30–31), Amos (5:18–20), and Zephaniah (1:14–15) use much the same language to describe the Day of the Lord, a day in history prophesied also by Jesus. Our Lord quoted the Isaiah passage, and said that after these signs the Son of Man will come in great power and glory and the angels will gather His people from all over the earth to meet Him in the air (Matt. 24:29–31).

Although there is the chance that this may happen in our lifetime, the second possibility is that we may die young, an eventuality rarely wished for by anyone. When people are hale and hearty they can occasionally be heard to assert that they hope they die before they grow old. But in actual fact most of us tenaciously cling to life no matter how infirm we become.

Death Is Certain

Unless the Lord's return does intervene, however, death is inevitable. The most comforting thing that can be said about death is that by it "man goes to his eternal home" (v. 5). Without the assurance from Jesus that He has prepared a place for us (John 14:1–2), our future would be grim indeed.

From an earthly point of view, dying is a wrenching business. Even poetic language cannot mask the violence incurred when the silver cord is *severed,* the golden bowl and wheel *broken,* the pitcher *shattered* (v. 6). No wonder Paul refers to death as man's enemy (1 Cor. 15:26), and no wonder in verse 5 Solomon speaks of mourners who go about in the streets! Death and decay are Satan's obscene alternatives to the life and beauty that God gives.

The Urgent Warning

But the point of Solomon's enumerations of the problems of old age is not to depress or drive to despair, but to warn. These verses are his urgent plea for people to reject man-made philosophies and turn to God. "Don't put it off," he cries. "Draw near to your Creator before it is too late. Remember your Creator before . . . before . . . before." Solomon knows that older people are often set in their ways, that they tend not to respond well to suggestions from others (Eccl. 4:13). Before people reach that state, he wants to say with Paul, "I tell you, now is the time of God's favor, now is the day of salvation'' (2 Cor. 6:2), and have them respond in faith before that day passes.

Those who think they will put off turning to God until they have "had their fun" are not thinking very clearly. Their silver cord may be severed before another day passes. Besides, God is not at the beck and call of man. We cannot snap our fingers and bring Him running to our death beds. Of what use are we to Him then? As one of David's servants said to him:

> I am now eighty years old. Can I tell the difference between what is good and what is not? Can your servant taste what he eats and drinks? Can I still hear the voices of men and women singers? Why should your servant be an added burden to my lord and king? (2 Sam. 19:35)

If we want our spirits to return to God who gave them, we must remember Him *before* our bodies return to the ground from which they came.

Age and Wisdom

Earlier in Ecclesiastes, Solomon labels the pursuit of wealth, pleasure, and possessions as futile and meaningless. This part of the twelfth chapter serves to illustrate the truth of that assertion. Where are the pleasures of food, drink, and sexual gratification now? How important are money and possessions if eyesight, hearing, and health are poor and a godless eternity is staring us in the face?

Of all the things examined by Solomon, only one survives the test of time, only one actually grows and improves with age, and that is wisdom. Even so, it is not earthly wisdom produced from "under the sun" that supremely benefits us and the young during our later years, but God's wisdom. As the psalmist reminds us, "The fear of the LORD is the beginning of wisdom; all who follow his precepts have good understanding" (Ps. 111:10). Those who have "remembered their Creator" have much of value to share, an important contribution to make to the people of God that does not end at age sixty-five. Experienced Christians, well versed in Scripture, are given the responsibility of training the next generation in the ways of the Lord:

> Likewise, teach the older women to be reverent in the way they live. . . . Then they can train the younger women to love their husbands and children, to be self-controlled and pure, to be busy at home, to be kind, and to be subject to their husbands, so that no one will malign the Word of God (Titus 2:3–5).

This kind of wisdom does not descend intact upon those who turn to God during their final days on earth, but is the product of years of study and fellowship with God. If we hope to have wisdom to share in our old age, we must not wait till we have one foot in the grave to begin to acquire it. Whatever our present age, if we want to be of use to God we must echo the prayer of Moses:

> The length of our days is seventy years—or eighty, if we have the strength. . . . Teach us to number our days aright, that we may gain a heart of wisdom (Ps. 90:10, 12).

* * * *

FINDING THE MEANING

1. What can an older person do when sleep is difficult? (See Psalm 63:6.) _____

   _____

2. What mistake can older people make in their dealings with others? (See Genesis 37:3–4.) _____

   _____

3. What can one expect to find in an older person? (See Job 12:12.) _____

   _____

4. What behavior is sometimes characteristic of widows? (See 1 Timothy 5:13.) _____

   _____

5. What comfort is there in the face of death? (See John 14:1–3.) _____

   _____

6. How is death actually an advantage to the one who believes in Christ? (See 1 Corinthians 15:42–44, 55–57.)

   _____

   _____

7. If Jesus were to return today, would you be one of the believers who would meet Him in the air? _____

   _____

8. What is your opinion of the older people you know? Are they improving with age? _____

   _____

   _____

9. What do you expect to be like when you are old? How do you plan to achieve this? _____

_____

_____

10. What can we learn from Ruth 1:1–7, 19–21, about our attitudes as we grow older? Compare with Job 1:14–22.

_____

_____

11. What is included in God's plan for older women? (See Titus 2:3–5.) _____

_____

_____

12. What is the trouble with age? _____

_____

_____

12

AVOIDING TROUBLE

Ecclesiastes 12:9–14

Solomon comes now to the close of his study of the ways people attempt to find meaning in life, the "heavy burden" borne by those who exclude God from their basic life plan (1:13). He wants to assure us that he has taken his role as teacher (1:12) seriously—so seriously, in fact, that the book was actually given that title: Ecclesiastes—the Teacher—the Preacher to the assembly of God's people. He has "pondered and searched out and set in order many proverbs. The Teacher searched to find just the right words, and what he wrote was upright and true" (12:9–10). He knows we were not always comfortable as our futile goals were exposed, for "the words of the wise are like goads" (v. 11), intended to prick our consciences. But he wants us to realize that whether we liked some of his teachings or not, God's truth, "like firmly embedded nails," must sink deep into our innermost being because it is "given by one Shepherd" (v. 11).

Solomon appears to be saying, "I realize that I told you at

the beginning that I was going to employ my own earthly wisdom to search out the meaning of life, and I did just that. My conclusion is that everything is futile without God. But now as I look back over what I have written, making sure every word and thought is just as it should be, I realize that I was guided all along by the Shepherd. *He* is the One who wanted you to know how vain all our efforts are apart from Him. What I have written is true. This is how we think, and our thinking is without meaning apart from God. Let this realization goad you into rejecting the vain thinking of man and trusting in the revealed truth of God."

Don't Trust Other Books

Solomon goes on to caution us not to trust in writing not given by the one Shepherd. "Be warned, my son, of anything in addition to them. Of making many books there is no end, and much study wearies the body" (v. 12). If this was true in Solomon's day, how much more so it is in ours!

Most modern-day cults produce one or more books that must be used by their followers along with the Bible, and that, in case of contradiction, supersede the Bible in authority. But God takes a dim view of any attempts to tamper with Scripture. In Deuteronomy 4:2, the Israelites were told, "Do not add to what I command you and do not subtract from it, but keep the commands of the LORD your God that I give you." The warning in Revelation 22:18–19 is even more awesome:

> I warn everyone who hears the words of the prophecy of this book: If anyone adds anything to them, God will add to him the plagues described in this book. And if anyone takes words away from this book of prophecy, God will take away from him his share in the tree of life and in the holy city, which are described in this book.

As Solomon said in Ecclesiastes 5:1–2, we must guard against spiritual error, and this includes the books we choose to aid us in our study of the Bible. There are those who twist Scripture to make it say what they want it to (2 Peter 3:16), and these people can write books and broadcast radio and television programs that appear legitimate. If we want to stay out of trouble, we will be on the alert to make sure our teachers neither *add* unbiblical ideas (even though they may be exciting ideas) nor *omit* some of the less popular teachings of Scripture, but who instead "correctly handle the word of truth" (2 Tim. 2:15).

I once began reading a novel by a prominent secular author that was based on the life of Paul. When I came upon the section that told of Paul's disillusionment with women because of his sexual relations with a fickle slave girl, I realized how hazardous that kind of reading is. Bible figures have no protection against blatant falsehoods concocted by modern writers: someone hundreds of years in the grave can hardly sue for libel! Contemporary novels on other themes are even more saturated with ungodly philosophies and immorality, especially sexual exploits that God condemns. There is no end of making books, but the Christian who wants to please his Shepherd will pick those he reads with care.

Law Vs. Grace

When Solomon writes of "the Shepherd," many of us automatically form an image of Jesus holding a lamb, and recall His statement, "I am the good shepherd. The good shepherd lays down his life for the sheep" (John 10:11). This, however, was not the picture in Solomon's mind, for he reigned one thousand years before the birth of Christ. His father, David, had also spoken of God as the Lord who was his shepherd (Ps. 23). But the God David and Solomon referred to was the God of Abraham, Isaac, and Jacob, the God who brought the Israelites out of Egypt and gave Moses the Law.

In Solomon's day, the faithful were forgiven of their sins

when they brought an animal to be killed to satisfy the death penalty incurred by their sins (Lev. 1:4 ff). Temple worship consisted of these virtually endless burnt offerings, public reading of Scripture and singing of psalms on special feast days, and various rituals performed daily by the priests that are recorded in detail in Exodus and Leviticus. The Jews of this time knew little about the Messiah who was to come, but kept the Law in obedience to God's command. "For the law was given through Moses; grace and truth came through Jesus Christ" (John 1:17).

Because Solomon lived so many years on the other side of the Cross, his summary cannot take into account the Christ who today saves from judgment those who trust in His death. Solomon came to God through the blood of bulls and goats, and never heard John say, as he pointed to Jesus, "Look, the Lamb of God, who takes away the sin of the world!" (John 1:29). He could not know of a final sacrifice for sin on a bloody cross. Nevertheless, since the Old Testament accounts "were written down as warnings for us, on whom the fulfillment of the ages has come" (1 Cor. 10:11), we would do well to consider carefully the closing counsel of this wise man of God if we want to avoid trouble today.

Fear God

As Solomon reaches "the conclusion of the matter," his first exhortation is: "Fear God" (v. 13). This, he says in Proverbs 1:7, is the first step to wisdom. Scripture speaks of the fear of the Lord scores of times as the proper attitude of creatures toward their Creator, whose works they can never understand (Eccl. 11:5). The fear of the Lord is a healthy awe that prevents us from behaving in an irreverent manner and causes us to be careful how we use any of God's many names. The fear of the Lord keeps us from viewing His judgment as a trifling matter and makes us grateful for the grace that allows us to be His friend. Above all, the fear of the Lord brings us to our knees in repentance as we realize that we deserve death for our sinful rebellion, and causes us to cry for mercy from the only one who can save us.

When we fear God, we can never worship the lesser gods of pleasure, materialism, human intellect, or status. We will instead have a wholesome hesitancy about wandering from His path because we know that the troubles He has predicted will certainly come if we do wander. A God who is mighty enough to inspire awe is the only God who will keep our attention from straying to the temptations of the world.

Keep His Commandments

The fear of the Lord is not supposed to paralyze us, but to motivate us to the kind of activity that pleases God: obeying His commandments. Jesus said, "If you love me, you will obey what I command" (John 14:15). If it seems odd that we are told to obey both from fear and from love, we need only recall that even on a human level respect is a prerequisite for real love. How much more worthy is our great God of the kind of love that makes us want to do His will!

The insistence on keeping God's commands is a continuous theme from Genesis to Revelation. People who call themselves Christians but do not obey God are fooling themselves (John 15:14). It is not enough simply to believe in the existence of God. "Even the demons believe that—and shudder" as they go about their hellish work (James 2:19). What proves that God is our personal God is our actual daily obedience to His will (James 2:14–18). Solomon says keeping God's commandments "is the whole duty of man" (12:13).

Nothing Can Be Hidden

Solomon's last word to us is the reminder that "God will bring every deed into judgment, including every hidden thing, whether it is good or evil" (v. 14). Paul also speaks of a time when each person's work "will be shown for what it is, because the Day will bring it to light" (1 Cor. 3:13). Christians accept the fact that we will have to give an account of ourselves to God, and trust in His grace and justice for the reward we deserve.

Non-Christians, however, do not view such a teaching so calmly. For the idea of a Day of Judgment contradicts and confounds every philosophy proposed by man. The existentialist says, "There is no absolute standard of right and wrong." God says, "Good and evil exist, and your deeds will be judged accordingly." The fatalist says, "It was my destiny, I couldn't help it." God says, "You are responsible for your actions. Every deed will be judged." The evolutionist says, "Man is only an animal. Animals don't know right from wrong." God says, "Man's spirit came from God. All your deeds will be brought into judgment." The atheist says, "There is no God." God says, "I AM, and I will bring every deed into judgment." The person with good intentions says, "I meant well. I did the best I could." God says, "The soul that sins will die. *Every* deed will be brought into judgment."

People who drift along in life, living morally on the surface but not committing themselves to God in their spirits are in no better condition than blatant sinners. Those who pretend to be Christians but have never asked God for forgiveness and put their faith in Christ are equally lost. "There is nothing hidden that will not be disclosed, and nothing concealed that will not be known or brought out into the open" (Luke 8:17). "Man looks at the outward appearance, but the LORD looks at the heart" (1 Sam. 16:7).

It is to the self-deluded that Solomon would direct his final words, to pseudo-believers about whom God said, "These people come near to me with their mouth and honor me with their lips, but their hearts are far from me. Their worship of me is made up only of rules taught by men" (Isa. 29:13). Jesus says that their hidden lack of faith will be brought to light at the judgment, and will earn trouble of the most eternal kind. At that time, He says, "Whoever has will be given even more; and whoever does not have, even what he thinks he has will be taken from him" (Luke 8:18).

Avoiding Trouble

Solomon has shown us the many roads that lead away from God and into trouble. He has revealed the dangers of each false way and condemned them as futile. He promises that the wisdom he has given will keep us out of trouble, will save us from "the ways of wicked men, from men whose words are perverse, who leave the straight paths to walk in dark ways, whose paths are crooked" (Prov. 2:12–15). And he urges us: "Trust in the LORD with all your heart and lean not on your own understanding; in all your ways acknowledge Him, and He will make your paths straight" (Prov. 3:5–6). For "I have seen all the things that are done under the sun; all of them are meaningless, a chasing after the wind" (Eccl. 1:14).

* * * *

FINDING THE MEANING

1. What does *Ecclesiastes* mean? _____

_____

_____

2. Why does Solomon never mention salvation through Jesus Christ? _____

_____

_____

3. What is the difference between the Old Testament covenant under which Solomon worshiped and the new covenant instituted by Jesus? (See 1 Corinthians 11: 23–25; Hebrews 9:11–15.) _____

_____

_____

4. What books have hindered rather than helped your spiritual growth? _____

_____

5. What gets us into trouble? (See Proverbs 15:27; 17:20; 22:24–25; 23:29–30; 24:2; 28:14.) _____

_____

_____

_____

6. Is the Christian promised freedom from all trouble? (See Psalm 90:10; Matthew 6:34; John 16:33; James 1:2–4.)

_____

_____

7. What confidence does the Christian have in the midst of trials? (See Psalm 32:7; 91:14–16; John 16:33.)

_____

_____

_____

8. What is the first good deed we must do? (See John 6:28–29.) _____

_____

_____

9. How will the good works of Christians be judged? (See 1 Corinthians 3:10–15.) _____

_____

10. How many of God's commandments for right living can you name? _____

_____

_____

_____

11. Which of the false philosophies presented in Ecclesiastes are most dangerous to you personally? _____

_____

_____

12. What can a person do to avoid getting into trouble?

_____

_____

NOTES

Chapter 2

[1]C. S. Lewis, *The Screwtape Letters* (New York: Macmillan, 1961), p. 49.
[2]Ibid., pp. 63–64.

Chapter 5

[1]Desmond Morris, *The Naked Ape* (New York: McGraw-Hill, 1967), p. 9.
[2]Ibid., p. 38.
[3]Ibid., p. 202.
[4]Ibid., p. 203.
[5]Ibid., pp. 208–9.
[6]Ibid., p. 9.
[7]Ibid., p. 39.
[8]Humanist Manifesto II, quoted in "Concerned Women for America Newsletter," P.O. Box 82957, San Diego, CA 92138, 1980.
[9]Hazel E. Barnes, *Humanistic Existentialism* (Lincoln, Neb.: University of Nebraska Press, 1967), p. 373.
[10]James W. Prescott and Douglas Wallace, "Abortion and the 'Right to Life': Facts, Fallacies, and Fraud," *The Humanist*, Nov.–Dec., 1978, pp. 36–39.
[11]Ibid.

[12]Joan Share, "The Makings of a Good Person," *The Humanist,* May–June 1981, pp. 30–31.

[13]Ibid.

[14]*Scientific Creationism,* classroom edition (San Diego, Calif.: Creation-Life, 1974), p. 141.

Chapter 6

[1]Hazel E. Barnes, *Humanistic Existentialism,* pp. 3, 369–70.

[2]Stanley Rosen, *Nihilism: A Philosophical Essay* (New Haven, Conn.: Yale University Press, 1969), p. 137.

[3]Francis Schaeffer, *Escape From Reason* (Downer's Grove, Ill.: Inter-Varsity, 1971), p. 7.

Chapter 8

[1]*Los Angeles Times,* Part I, p. 10, August 6, 1981.

[2]*Los Angeles Times,* Part V, p. 7, June 17, 1981.

Chapter 10

[1]James C. Dobson, *Straight Talk to Men and Their Wives* (Waco, Texas: Word, 1980), p. 147.